I Was a
Potato Oligarch

For Nuala, who is still amused.

*And for Vladimir, Alex and Malcolm,
who made the Big Idea possible.*

*With grateful thanks to Pippa Roberts and Neil McFarland,
who turned sketches into pictures.*

*And to Nick Brealey, Sally Lansdell, Angie Tainsh and
Victoria Fedorowicz, who made a book out of a script.*

I Was a Potato Oligarch

Travels and Travails in the New Russia

John Mole

NICHOLAS BREALEY
PUBLISHING

LONDON · BOSTON

First published by
Nicholas Brealey Publishing in 2008

3–5 Spafield Street
Clerkenwell, London
EC1R 4QB, UK
Tel: +44 (0)20 7239 0360
Fax: +44 (0)20 7239 0370

20 Park Plaza, Suite 1115A
Boston
MA 02116, USA
Tel: (888) BREALEY
Fax: (617) 523 3708

www.nicholasbrealey.com
www.johnmole.com

The right of John Mole to be identified as the author of this
work has been asserted in accordance with the Copyright,
Designs and Patents Act 1988.

Illustrations by the author, Pippa Roberts & Neil McFarland.

ISBN: 978-1-85788-509-5

British Library Cataloguing in Publication Data
A catalogue record for this book is available from the
British Library.

Printed in the UK by Clays Ltd on
Forest Stewardship Council certified paper.

FSC

Contents

This is the Big One

I had my Russian Big One in a sauna on a missile base outside Moscow. When I have a great idea that is certain to make us rich I say to the family, "This is the Big One." There have been many Big Ones over the years, all of which have shrunk into Little Ones.

That afternoon I was with my friend Misha, suffering fifteen minutes of torture in the hot room before going back to the main purpose of the afternoon, a pigeon and mushroom hotpot and a litre of vodka. We had already worked through several varieties of smoked sturgeon, a wild boar sausage and a dish of fresh vegetables, flown in from the south by military aircraft. The base commander had a sideline in hiring out planes to the Chechen traders who monopolized the city markets.

"So, John, what do you think of our poor Russia?"

"I love it, Meesh. I've never known anything like it. It's revolution. Anything is possible. Everything is changing. There's such energy."

"It is frenzy of fear. For you change is always good. For us change is always bad. *To an optimist bedbugs smell like cognac. To a pessimist cognac smells like bedbugs.*"

"Whatever. I wish I could get stuck in. It's so exciting."

He picked up a bucket of ice-cold water. I knew what he was going to do with it and I was keen to say something that would make him stop. I don't like saunas. I don't like the heat, the burning lungs, the eyes stinging with sweat, the hot wood on my bottom. I don't like staccato conversation made inane by the stewing of brains. I don't like macho men daring each other to pour water on the stove. And I especially don't like them pouring it over my head.

"Misha, wait. I have an idea for a business. It's a brilliant idea."

It worked. He put the bucket down on his knee. I had to keep talking long enough for him to forget the water.

"What's Russia famous for?"

"*Znachet*, caviar." *Znachet* was a verbal tic, the equivalent of *I mean* or *I guess*.

"Close."

"Vodka."

"Not what I'm thinking of."

"Tchaikovsky. Dostoevsky."

"Get back to food."

"Cabbage."

"Closer. What goes with cabbage?"

"*Cabbage soup and kasha, food for Russia.*" *Kasha* is buckwheat porridge, like semolina or American grits. The word alone was enough to start my stomach heaving.

"Potatoes. Russia grows a third of the world's potatoes."

"I must tell you there are already many people in potato growing business. *Znachet*, most of population."

★

"I wasn't thinking of growing them. I was thinking of selling them."

"Sell potatoes to Russians? Why not snow to Eskimos? *You don't go to Tula with your samovar.*"

"The British answer to McDonald's and Pizza Hut is baked potatoes. In their skin with cheese or baked beans or salad or stew. Potatoes are just a base for the filling. It's one of my favourites."

"You are half Irish."

"Cut the stereotypes. You know who eats the most potatoes in Europe?"

"Germany."

"Portugal. They eat as many per head as Russians."

"*Znachet*, no Russian will go out for a potato. They can have that at home."

"They can have chopped meat on a bun at home too. Russians don't go to McDonald's for the food, they go for a slice of the West. Let's open a baked potato restaurant. A taste of Britain. Tradition, sophistication, elegance, bobbies outside the door, servers in bowler hats, cricket bats on the wall…

"…warm beer, rain, football hooligans…"

"…pictures of the Queen…"

"…and Fatcher…"

I would rather have a blown-up colour photo of a salmonella bug in my restaurant than Her, but I let the comment pass. I wiped my sweaty face on my sodden sheet. At least in a Russian sauna you are spared nudity. Some men tie their sheet over their shoulder like a toga. Some tie it

3

over their breasts like a woman coming out of the shower. Others tuck it under their bellies like Sumo wrestlers. I favour Death of Socrates, under the breasts and over the belly. I had to keep talking.

"Everything is natural. Cheese and butter and sour cream and salad. And for the hot sauces we take a Russian stew and jazz it up with curry. Traditional English."

"*Znachet,* where is the gimmick? Where is the difference?"

"The staff could smile at the customers. That would be a Unique Selling Proposition." Russians smile a lot but not in front of strangers.

"The customers will think they are idiots."

"Here's the gimmick. You'll love this, Misha. We'll make it a franchise operation. Individuals. Mom and Pop. Cooperatives. Anyone. You're in the small-business business, you tell me how it works."

"In Russia it will be very difficult."

"You get paid to tell people how easy it is. Put your money where your mouth is. Pull this off and you can keep yourself in conferences for years. You might even get rich."

"On potatoes?"

"It's not potatoes, Misha, it's the value added. The concept. The image. We're dealing in aspirations. We're dealing in dreams."

"Russians have had enough of dreams and aspirations. We had seventy years of them."

"I don't mean the Russians. I mean the do-gooders in the West. The Eurocrats. The Bureaucrats. Brussels. The

British Know-How Fund. Soros. We'll have grants and sub-sidies coming out of our ears. Think of the feasibility stud-ies. I sniff per diems in this, Misha. Per diems. So what do you think?"

"*Znachet*, not a snowball's chance."

He scowled into the bucket of water and tossed it onto the stove, where it exploded into steam. I hate that, but I had avoided the douche. And he liked the idea. If Russians tell you something is a good idea you might as well forget it. They're not taking it seriously. You want them to say it will be very, very difficult, full of insurmountable risks and problems. Then you know they are really considering it. Pessimism is not just a Russian attitude, it is a deeply ingrained conviction of how the world works.

"The beauty is we don't have to worry about raw mate-rials. In a baked potato restaurant *all we have to do is pick the potatoes out of the fields.* They go straight in the oven and we serve them. We don't even peel them."

The words in italics are chiselled into my conscience, along with all the other stupidities that make me bite my pillow in the middle of the night. If only I could have eaten them there and then.

How did I get here? I was down on my luck. My invest-ments and business capers had flopped. My latest novel was submerged in rejection slips. Newspaper editors didn't return my calls, not even those from the back pages of the appointments sections. My only book still in print, *Mind Your Manners* about how to manage cross-cultural difference in Europe, was doing well, selling several thousand copies a year, but with a royalty of about a pound a book it hardly covered the mortgage. What could I do? Go out to work? When I resigned from a bank to be a writer I made a solemn vow: Never Again. I had no professional qualifications and no marketable skills. There was always management consulting, but I'd rather go minicabbing.

Fate stepped in. I wangled a press pass to a conference on private enterprise in Eastern Europe to gather material about emerging business cultures in the new democracies. The tables and graphs in the document pack were lies. The speeches were dull. I needed an anecdote, a human interest story. Little did I know I was about to start my own.

Among the double-breasted bankers, single-breasted salesmen and academics in sports jackets that hadn't been buttoned over their breasts since they were assistant lecturers, one block-headed man stood out in jeans and boots and a brown leather jacket. I hadn't seen his like since I bought caviar outside the Aurora hotel in St Petersburg in the days of the dying Chernenko. It wasn't so much the clothes but the street corner stance, the way he sized up the rest of us, looking for a way in. I walked up to him and squinted at his name tag. Right first time, a Russian with an international company. I offered him my coffee.

"*Znachet*, what is your profession?" he asked.

"I write about business cultures."

He squinted at my name tag and his eyes opened wide. "You are John Mole? *The* John Mole?"

There's John Mole the poet and John Mole the Catholic apologist, John Mole the bassist and John Mole the expert on structural weakness in suspension bridges. So I can't claim the definite article.

"*A* John Mole, certainly."

He beamed a gold-glinting smile and seized my hand. "Very fine! We use your book in our training."

"What? Where?"

"In Russia."

To my knowledge there was no Russian edition. "Which part do you use?"

"The whole thing. It is required reading in our syllabus."

"Who publishes it?"

"Mr Xerox."

An honour. My work circulated in *samizdat*, clandestine copies of suppressed literature. In the old days it was *Doctor Zhivago* and *One Day in the Life of Ivan Denisovitch*. Now it was books with titles like *How to Read the Financial Pages* and *Principles of Marketing*. Nice for me, but I felt a pang of nostalgia.

"Don't let my publisher hear that. He'll sue."

He laughed. "In Russia? Let him try."

We exchanged cards. His title was Small Business Consultant and he was based in Rome. By the end of the coffee break we were Misha and John. We went back into the auditorium together, sat at the back and filled our minds with privatization in the Polish retail industry, share coupons in the Czech Republic and the private bus network in Bulgaria. It was like meditation, purging the mind of the cares of life and filling it with sublime vacuousness. We queued together for quiche.

"I have an idea," he said. "You will come to Russia and make lectures. We will organize it."

"Who is we?" I asked.

"*Znachet*, our group. We have training and investment and marketing consultancy." He gave me another business card that proclaimed ICBM – International Consultancy and Business Management, with addresses in Moscow, London, Rome and New York.

"I thought you were with…"

"ICBM is private business."

"How much will you pay?"

"Don't worry. We will make you millionaire."

"Sounds good."

"*Znachet*, a rouble millionaire."

"It's a start."

We shook hands with many expressions of goodwill and expectations for future cooperation and other international trade mission sentiments. I worked the room separately for the rest of the lunch break, took an afternoon nap in the back row and slipped away at tea time to catch the half-price early showing at the Ritzy. Misha had disappeared too. I put the idea of a lecture tour of Russia on a par with "let's do lunch". So I was surprised three days later to be faxed a formal invitation from ICBM to make a five-week tour of Russia, Ukraine and Belarus, all expenses paid plus 50 per cent of the engagement fees. It beat minicabbing.

Refugees in their own country

The flight to Moscow was full. Ruddy oil men, City money launderers, scrubbed Mormon missionaries, fleshy Russian bankers, po-faced lawyers, earnest human rights watchers, sad Russians abandoning children in English schools, self-important journalists, introverted scientists poring over papers, solemn Eurocrats, excited exchange students, fact-finding MPs, air-mile-clocking businessmen, boozing, reading, talking, laptopping. I felt at home in this airship of fools kept aloft by the hope of gain in the chaos of Yeltsin's Russia.

At the airport Misha picked me out of the maul. He seemed as relieved to see me as I was to see him. We had fixed up my visit in one casual meeting in London and a couple of faxes and neither of us was sure the other was serious. Not that we were effusive. Russians are as inhibited as Brits in public displays. While he fetched the car I practised my Russian on the leather-jacketed toughs touting taxis in the blizzard outside. *Nyet.*

Misha's car was a silver Volvo estate with stickers witnessing a career in Switzerland before promotion to serious winters. It had all the basics, while bits of wire and string took care of incidentals like door handles. After reassuring each other of the satisfactoriness of my journey, conversation lapsed on the motorway into town. I resorted to the banker's ploy of asking how the rouble was doing. While he rabbited on about budgets and inflation and the price of petrol, I gawped out of the window. Potholes, black slush, massive trucks belching diesel, ramshackle hoardings, overhead cables, a general air of impermanence and improvisation and large-scale tawdriness – it reminded me of America.

We arrived at an apartment complex near Dynamo stadium. Unpointed red brick, metal doors, graffiti, cars from a wrecker's yard; broken paths, old grass, mud ponds, scuttering leaves; dark figures trudging through the dusk, pointy-headed in ski hats, round-shouldered in anoraks; chill wind and phlegmy gobs of rain; no street lights, the odd bare bulb in a doorway. Misha hefted my bag on his shoulder and punched a number into the keypad on the door. I followed him into the lobby with my briefcase and slide projector, the asset of our enterprise.

It was like a squat. Broken lamps, peeling paint, dilapidated concrete staircase. Cats had crapped in some dark corner. We squeezed into a phone booth of a lift without a light and rattled in darkness to the sixth floor. The door to the flat was a slab of raw steel with spot-welded hinges and a keyhole burned out with an oxy torch. Set in the middle was an ornate brass door knocker.

"*Znachet*, they break down wooden doors with axes," said Misha, hammering the knocker like a bailiff.

The door swung open and inside was light and warmth and tobacco and cabbage and wax and struggling lemon freshener. I stuck out my hand to a thin man in black sweater, black jeans and black-rimmed spectacles, who said he was Oleg. Misha pushed me inside before I could commit the Russian sin of stepping on the threshold or shaking hands over it, but I took my shoes off without being prompted. I was rewarded with a pair of fleecy pink slippers. Compulsory slipper wearing is a great leveller. Whether you're in a designer cocktail dress or Savile Row suit or Armani casuals, it's hard to stand on ceremony in fluffy slippers.

A woman appeared, wiping her hands on a tea towel, Oleg's wife Olga. She was older than Oleg, mid-40s, the northern type of Russian, big boned, blonde hair, blue eyes slightly slant, swathed in fluffy lilac cashmere and pungent scent. She was shy and embarrassed. I was the first foreigner in her flat.

Olga led us straight to the table in the living room. It was loaded with *zakuska*, cold hors d'oeuvres, several different kinds of ham, sausage, smoked sturgeon and salmon, salads, black caviar and red caviar, cheese, potatoes, little pies and flans. Vodka, Moldovan white wine and watery fruit juice were on offer, but I was expected to join the others in a glass of Italian Amaretto, the sophisticated Muscovite's choice at the time. It was like liquid marzipan, so I tossed it back like medicine. This was ill-mannered since I did not wait for the toast of welcome, and ill-advised because Oleg immediately refilled my glass with the horrible stuff.

Oleg was a subeditor at *Izvestia* and freelanced for the *Moscow Business Times*. The rest of his name was Josef Santana and he was the grandson of one of the thousands of Spanish communists who fled to Odessa at the end of the Spanish civil war. His looks and his name were his only Hispanic legacy. After marrying a Russian girl, his grandfather went to South America when Stalin's pact with Hitler extinguished his last hopes for European Communism. Oleg spent his spare time learning Spanish and trying to track down his grandparents' birth and marriage certificates, which he hoped would give him Spanish citizenship and a passport to the West.

Olga was notionally employed by the economic planning department of the ministry of transport and spent her working day selling cashmere sweaters at her pitch in front of the Belaruskaya railway station. She worked for a "shuttler", a woman who shuttled between Moscow and Istanbul or Dubai buying stuff to sell in the street.

Their son Petya came in. He wore a startlingly white trenchcoat and carried a satellite phone, like a car battery with a handset on top. He could have modelled for a Hero of the USSR poster in front of a combine harvester. Chiselled good looks, cheerful, blond, muscular, his mother's son, not a gene of Oleg to be seen; from which I concluded that he was the fruit of a previous marriage. As 80 per cent of Russian marriages end in divorce, it was a reasonable assumption. He was a student at an engineering school, where his uncle was a lecturer in motorway repair. Confident of excellent grades because of his family connection, Petya spent his time selling satellite phones for an American company.

"You all have second jobs," I said.

"*Znachet*, these are first jobs," said Misha. "How else do we survive? In Soviet times we said 'we pretend to work and they pretend to pay us'. Now nobody pretends. Ten dollars a month is good salary. Many people have not received salary for six months. And when they do it is worth nothing. Inflation is 100 per cent a month. If you get roubles you turn them immediately into dollars. Dollar is our currency now."

"God help them if they have pensions," said Oleg.

"How do people live? Those who can't get dollars?"

"They get food parcels from America and Europe. We are refugees in our own country," said Olga.

"We have no country, Mama," said Petya. "We were citizens of the Soviet Union. It does not exist now."

"Russia is our country," said Misha.

"And the Russians in the republics? Their homeland became a foreign country."

We tucked in. This time I waited for the toasts. In private or public they followed the same pattern: Welcome – The Ladies – Friends – Peace – Prosperity. The food was delicious and I managed to swap the Amaretto for vodka. The others drank fruit juice. Alcohol consumption in Russia is famous and is blamed for the low male life expectancy, but the young professional middle classes and scientists I mixed with hardly drank anything. Women did not drink at all. If you were driving it was automatically assumed that you would be on fruit juice all night. So some people must be getting more than their ration. Foreign businessmen complain that their Russian hosts deliberately get them drunk. We Brits don't need much encouragement and we make the mistake of drinking between toasts. For once I didn't, so by London standards it was a sober evening.

After dinner Oleg and Misha took me to Red Square. It was deserted. The rain had stopped and it was a clear, moonlit night. The last time I was here it was the Heart of the Evil Empire. And now? The alien, sinister, threatening mystique had evaporated along with the Soviet Union. The red ruby stars on the towers and spires looked pretty. St Basil's was a fairytale confection. The Kremlin walls were quaint. At midnight soldiers marched a silly goosestep to Lenin's tomb and replaced the two standing guard at the door.

A beautiful woman in a fur hat came up to us. She offered us postcards. She said she was a schoolteacher and lived with her invalid mother. We bought cards and she offered us a map of Moscow. We bought the map and then she offered to come back to our hotel and sleep with us. Misha gave her five dollars and we wished her good night.

The New Russia?

ICBM had a staff of two, Misha and Oleg. The world head-quarters was the alcove in Olga and Oleg's bedroom where they kept the computer. We planned our mission. Oleg perched on the dressing table, Misha sprawled on the bed, I had the honour of the bedroom chair.

ICBM's primary activity was selling management training courses in Rome to managers of Russian companies. The companies paid 15,000 dollars. Training was provided free under a European aid programme. The trainees received a 5000-dollar cashback to take home. After travel and accommodation were paid for, the rest was profit to ICBM. Not a bad little business if you could find the punters – which is where I came in. The lecture tour of the world-famous international management guru John Mole targeted companies in privatization. *Izvestia* and the *Moscow Business Times* would advertise extensively before and give glowing reports after, thanks to Oleg.

"*Znachet*, the Small Business Adviser will make welcome and introduction. He will keep it short. Half an hour. Professor John Mole the savant from England and America will make presentation. Two hours. Then Chairman of ICBM will conclude."

"Two hours! That's too long."

"It is really one hour. We have a consecutive interpretation." This meant that we took it in turns to speak.

"Do we have an interpreter?"

"Of course. This is quality status project. We have European grants for administrator, interpreter, seminar chairman, main speaker, audiovisual expert and driver."

"I know who the main speaker is, but who are the others?"

"That is Misha, Misha, Misha, Oleg and Oleg," said Oleg, counting off the jobs on his fingers.

"They are expensive but very good and Brussels can afford it," said Misha. It was nice to hear that some of the aid was ending up in the pockets of Russians instead of Western consultants and the luxury hotels they stayed in.

"What do I get out of it?" I asked.

"All expenses. Half receipts on the door. For public presentations this will be in roubles, very sorry. But for the company presentations you will receive five dollars for every person who comes."

"You're charging them ten dollars to listen to me? That's a week's salary."

"Their companies pay twenty dollars."

"Twenty dollars! That's criminal! ... Hey, why don't I get ten dollars?"

"They get a cashback for themselves of ten dollars."

"You're bribing them to come. With their own company's money."

"They will not come. They will take cashback and send their deputies."

★

"This is absurd."

"This is Russia."

"The New Russia."

"No. Same old Russia in new clothes."

Our first gig was at the Central Russian House of Knowledge, a grey-stone mansion near Lubyanka Square. It had been built by one of the great aristocratic families of St Petersburg, the Chertkovs. After the Revolution it became a public lecture hall for the enlightenment of the people. Grainy pictures of previous lecturers adorned the staircase wall. Cocktail Molotov, Park Gorky, Ballet Kirov and many other famous names had trod the boards.

"You know Kirov?" asked Misha. "Stalin had him killed because he was too popular. He was famous for affairs with ballerinas. Stalin named the ballet company after him. It was his joke."

We had a poster outside in the street and puffs in *Izvestia* and the *Moscow Business Times*. How to Make Successful Business in Europe. Tickets were a thousand roubles, about fifty pence. We sold only two, but Misha told me not to worry. By four o'clock they would be queuing round the block. When we got there our room on the first floor was occupied. Two hundred people, mainly men in army uniforms, listened to a little man in a grey polyester suit lecturing too close to the mike on strategies for dealing with retirement.

"Poor bastards," said Misha. "With their pensions they'll spend their retirement selling doughnuts on the street."

The lavatories were so disgusting that I was cured for ever of having to take half a dozen leaks before I get on the podium. I hung round the landing outside our room adjusting my tie and patting my hair under a massive mural of Lenin reading a ticker tape. He looked like a Belgian dentist checking his stocks. At last the army trooped out, each with a black plastic briefcase and looking gloomy. They called each other *tavarish*, comrade, which boded ill for adjustment to civilian life under capitalism.

I set up the projector, adjusted the screen, fiddled with my notes, took a deep breath. We were in the aptly name Hall of Mirrors. Not only the walls but the pillars and the ceiling were mirrored. When I nodded my head, seventeen other John Moles nodded their heads. It looked like the only audience I was going to get. As the seconds dragged on to four o'clock, I went over to where Misha and Oleg were quietly arguing.

"Shall we wait for our two ticket holders to show up?"

"*Znachet*, they're here. Oleg and I bought them to get the ice moving."

"Oh great. Let's go home."

"We can't. We have camera crew. National network. You will be famous all over Russia."

"I hope they don't want audience reaction shots."

"Don't worry," said Oleg, "*The first pancake is always a blob.*"

Misha went out into the street to round up a studio audience. He came back with a few dispirited men in anoraks and ski hats, a woman in a red coat with her head entirely swathed like the Invisible Man in a white woolly scarf, a couple of stragglers from the previous lecture with red-banded army hats pushed back on their heads like halos, a cleaning lady in grey overalls still fingering the ten rouble note Misha had slipped her. To make up the front row we had half a dozen characters from *War and Peace*: a hussar with a red jacket over one shoulder, a pretty girl in ball gown and wig, a count in a blue uniform with medals and stars, a bishop with a tall black hat. They were all replicated by the mirrors into a vast green room of extras for a Brechtian epic.

"They launch a book here afterwards," whispered Misha, "about Tsar Nicholas."

"How can I keep a straight face?"

"Think of your dead mother."

"My mother's not dead."

"Even better."

The crew from Channel Three arrived. They wanted excerpts of the presentation and an interview. Television crews the world over seem to treat everything you say as pretentious garbage while the big black eye peers into your face for your innermost misgivings. How to Make Successful Business in Europe? If I knew, I wouldn't have to be doing this.

While I was nervous, Misha was magisterial. He delivered a fifteen-minute monologue to the camera on the need for international management education and ICBM's mission to deliver it.

The rest of the event was excruciating. I went into my routine, pausing at the end of each sentence for Misha to translate. I am not an inspiring public speaker at the best of times, but delivered in staccato bursts I was even more stilted than usual. It must have been worse for any poor devil who understood English, since they had to listen to it twice. While Misha spoke to the camera I looked down at the gloomy faces staring at the backs of the heads in front and wondered what on earth all this meant to them. Might as well talk about business on the moon. I reassured myself that this was the conventional demeanour of a Soviet audience at a lecture. Speeches were not meant to inform or entertain, but to reinforce the status of the speaker and the right of the audience to be included in the group. The event itself was an opportunity for private meditation or sleep. This is how I rationalized it over the desultory applause and the rush for the exit.

"How did it go?" I asked at the end, hoarse and perspiring with excessive adrenaline.

"Great," said Misha. "They will put it out nationwide. Minsk to Vladivostok, Archangel to Odessa. ICBM is launched, my friend."

One of the audience, an undernourished little man in a tired dark suit, pallid shirt and washed-out red tie introduced himself as the manager of the building. Mine was the last lecture at the House of Knowledge. Tomorrow the builders moved in to renovate it. The rumour was that Luzhkov, the Mayor of Moscow, would take it back for receptions and dinners. I was moved. I felt I had made a fitting contribution to the history of the place. From the Dawn of Communism to the Dusk of Free Market

Capitalism. The Fathers of the Revolution must have turned in their niches in the Kremlin wall.

I needed a drink. Oleg was putting the stuff in the car. Misha was schmoozing the television crew and slipping them dollar bills. Under the mural of Lenin catching up on the news stood two weedy youths dressed up as Tsarist Cossacks guarding the entrance to the book launch. They refused anyone not wearing a tie. This included a few soon-to-be-retired Red Army officers still hanging around with plastic briefcases and podgy necks liberated by unbuttoned collars. I breezed through the clash of Red and White Armies. Book launches mean booze. The refreshment in question was demi-sec *shampanskoe*, a sweet and fruity alcopop, not to be confused with champagne after which it is named. The bouquet is like the sweet cider I used to puke up on the doorstep when I came home from teenage parties, but it was nectar after my trying afternoon.

The room was eighteenth century, chandeliers in the plaster ceiling, a parquet floor, lovely pastel blues and pinks and ochres mellowed by time and tobacco smoke. My *War and Peace* extras loitered in a self-conscious huddle in front of an ornate marble fireplace. The rest of the guests were the seedy mixture of book launch freeloaders you find the world over, groping alternately for the drinks tray and each other and avoiding the subject of books.

A tall, skinny, baby-faced man in his best suit and black hair plastered down like a bathing cap stood swigging *shampanskoe* by a small table of books between two windows. He must have been the author, wondering whose party this really was and why nobody wanted to buy a signed copy. Out of professional solidarity I went over to him. I arrived just after a blowsy middle-aged woman, dressed for a gala première in a fifties lamé cocktail dress and jangling jewellery. They looked at me as if I had burst into the bedroom.

"Congratulations," I said and raised my glass. He gave me a nervous little nod while she graciously put out her hand for me to shake. With a little bow I brought the acrylic lace glove to within a breath of my lips, Polish style. I couldn't think of anything to say, so reached between them for a book and flicked through the black-and-white photographs in the middle. As far as I could tell through the haze of poor-quality printing, they were pictures of smoking factories alternating with portraits of the Romanovs. The last picture was a steam locomotive with a cow catcher on the front festooned with bunting. A gravelly voice interrupted my browsing and I turned instinctively to the man. It was the woman speaking.

"It is the history of industrialization under the Tsars. It is clear that if the Revolution of 1917 had been defeated, Russia would by now have an economy more powerful than America."

"Yes," said the man. He had a high-pitched, fluting voice, as if the dubbing had got them mixed up. "Look at the Trans-Siberian railway. It was planned to link Paris with New York via a bridge over the Bering Strait."

It wasn't my kind of book. Not enough conversation, as Alice would say. Might-have-been alternative universes are done better by science fiction. But I was still at the early stage of a stay in a foreign country when you are eager to ingratiate yourself with the natives. In any case, having gone through the ordeal myself, I have the utmost admiration for anyone who has written a book, whether it's a history of Sanskrit literature, a Mills & Boon romance or a guide to growing runner beans.

"How much is it?" I asked. Gratitude stole over his worried face.

"Only two thousand roubles," she said.

"I've got no roubles. Will ten dollars do?"

It certainly would. In no time at all I was relieved of the crisp greenback. It would have paid for twenty copies, but I took only one. Solidarity with fellow authors and all that. We exchanged little bows and I drifted back into the pool looking for another slug of *shampanskoe* before I rejoined Misha. Clutching my book I felt I belonged in literary Moscow. On the way out I was stopped by a chubby young woman in a red dress. She pointed at the book.

"Those are for sale," she said.

"I know. I bought one."

"I do not think so. Where is the receipt?"

"I bought it from the author."

"The author died last year."

I looked wildly round for the living author and his gravel-voiced companion. Not a hope. They had done a runner with the equivalent of a week's wages. This time I forked out five dollars to the lady in red. Misha gave me a telling off for disappearing. The *shampanskoe* gave me a headache.

To mark our first presentation, we called on the Father of the Revolution, Vladimir Ilyich Lenin, in his tomb before the Kremlin Wall in Red Square. He lay in a glass case in front of a sarcophagus in a dimly lit room decorated with scarlet zigzags, evoking the triumph of the Red Revolution or the fires of hell, depending on your point of view. This is how the travel writer Robert Byron described him in 1930, in *First Russia Then Tibet*: "Lenin must have been a very small man…" Fifty years later the great Colin Thubron wrote in *Among the Russians*: "Lenin lay there bigger than I imagined..." To me he looked about the right size. He had changed out of khaki army uniform into civvies shortly before the Great Patriotic War. His banker's suit and white spotty tie are refreshed every three years, and he gets an annual medical.

Outside in Red Square, Misha was scathing. "The cause of all our troubles."

"So you're not an old Communist."

"*Znachet*, of course I am Communist. We are all Communists. What else do we know? Do you think New Russians came down from the moon? *Every year the wolf sheds his hair but remains grey*. This does not mean we are stupid. See the flag there on Kremlin? Russian flag. We have Russian Independence Day now on June 12. Independence from who? From ourselves? It is a nonsense. We must change. *Moscow was not built in a day*. I will show you where I found my liberation. It is nice walk."

As we left Red Square, Misha pointed out his favourite sights: the window of the apartment where Stalin died, the red stars on top of the Kremlin towers made of Siberian rubies, the manhole padlocked against homeless children who lived in the sewers. We turned sharp left along the Kremlin wall down the Alexander Garden, to the tomb of the Unknown Soldier. It was a square of granite in front of an altar with a bronze helmet and banner. In the centre of the square a flame flickered out of a five-pointed star.

"Please, take hands out of pockets. This is sacred to all Russians. On day of their wedding couples come for their photograph here. You know the biggest feast day in Russia?"

"First of May? Revolution Day?"

"Victory Day. The defeat of Fascism in Great Patriotic War. It was the greatest thing Russia did for the world. Not Lenin."

"I think we gave you some help."

"We fought from Moscow to the Elbe. Two thousand kilometres. You came from English Channel. Six hundred kilometres. We lost twenty million dead. One fifth of population. How many did you lose?"

I pondered the flame while he bought us ice creams from a vendor. I pondered the icy blob of invisible bacilli.

"Should we eat ice cream here?"

"Eat for the dead."

As we walked on, I managed to flick mine from the cone into the gutter while Misha pointed out the Manezh, a great classical riding academy that was now an exhibition hall.

"The Communists used it as garage for the ZILs of the *nomenklatura*," he said. "Now they sell Mercedes and Chryslers."

Past the Manezh he pointed over the road to another classical building, the imposing Lenin Library, fronted with columns and topped with statues. After the collapse of the Soviet Union it was ceremonially renamed the Russian State Library, but His name was still over the door and on its metro station. We crossed the road. Misha ran up the marble steps and patted the plinth of Dostoevsky on the way to the library entrance. This was puzzling. How had Misha found liberation in a library? Books are my escape hatch, but I did not associate Misha with the parallel universes of literature.

Misha had a reader's card and it was the work of a moment and a passport to get a day pass for me. Inside the hall was an impressive staircase going up to a vast landing lit by crystal chandeliers and full of card-index cabinets. It was reassuringly like every other great library: the lovely musty smell, floor polish, whispered conversations of readers and the loud voices librarians permit themselves. Misha knocked a knuckle on the side of a catalogue.

"This was big lie. Harmless books and propaganda."

He led the way to another landing and down a wide circular staircase to the bowels of the library, all too literally. An unpleasant stench floated up the stairwell: stale piss, fresh shit, bad drains and the sort of disinfectant that brings out the aroma like lemon juice on strawberries. I held my breath, which prevented me asking where we were going, other than the obvious. Before we reached the toilets Misha pushed open a dark-painted door stating "no entry – staff only" in gold letters.

"In old days policeman sat here. This is real library. If we are stopped, you are from British Library. Look important."

We walked down long, cream-painted corridors and through swinging fire doors to a small lobby with narrower corridors leading off.

"Here was another guard. He examined all my papers. I needed special clearance from library, from university, from ministry and from KGB. It was one year to get these papers."

Twenty yards down one of the corridors Misha flung open a door, switched on the light and stood aside to let me pass. It was like an interrogation cell. Peeling green walls, a neon centre light, a metal table. The door had a spy hatch. It was warm and fusty, but I shuddered.

"*Znachet*, this is where I make my PhD."

"You said it was in business management."

"Of course. Very dangerous science. They locked you in. You pushed button to go out. They took very long to come. I bring in piss bottle just in case."

"What on earth were you studying?"

"I make first thesis in Soviet Union on small business management."

"Dangerous stuff."

"You laugh. It was a big risk for me. I could not tell nobody about my work. When I defended my thesis they locked the door. Only me and professors. They knew nothing about management so I had no problems. The next day I applied for posting to international organizations. I was not foreign ministry or *nomenklatura*, but they wanted someone who knew what Americans were talking about. It was my liberation. It started here."

"What were you reading?"

"*BusinessWeek, Management Today, Fortune.* Tom Peters' *In Search of Excellence* was my bible."

"Did you research private Russian companies?"

"And be killed by mafia? Only my professor knew what I was doing and he was afraid for me. It was a hard work. But times are different. We are out of jail now. We should make money."

Biznismyen

Everyone in Russia wanted to make money, whether to survive or get rich. For the poorest, the pensioners, the jobless, the unpaid, it was scarcely more than begging. In Yekaterinburg we bought up one old *babushka*'s entire stock, a left shoe. For the rest it seemed like the explosion of pent-up desire. They sold necessities and also the luxury, the aspirational, the quirky, the worthless and the useless, bought and sold for the pleasure of trading that had been denied for three generations. Shoppers thronged in stadiums and squares, stations, streets and subways. For every seller there were ten people inspecting the merchandise. Nobody wanted roubles. You paid with dollars or Marlboro.

"*Znachet*, someone should make thesis. Oldest profession in world is not whore, it is shop assistant."

A lot of this activity was making public what had been going on in secret for years. In the Time of Stagnation things were rationed by scarcity. Everyone carried a string bag, a "just in case", for when they came across something – anything – to buy. Window shopping was meaningless; there was nothing in the windows. Instead, you spent your shopping time in queues. Companies provided shops for their employees and stocked them with stuff they made or grew themselves, the surpluses traded with other companies. The black market in goods and favours flourished, from getting a *dacha* to a university place. Sweeteners, grease, bribes oiled the system. But it was always private, overtly frowned on. *Biznismyen* was a term of abuse.

The same thing was happening on a larger scale in industry. Raw materials, industrial goods, inventories were bought for a song or appropriated or simply stolen and then exported or sold on. Licences for oil and gas and minerals and forests were shared out and traded. Managers colluded with politicians and party members to hive off the going concerns among the vast conglomerates and leave the rest to be shored up by the state. Government monopolies became private monopolies defended by political patronage or murder. Assets went not to the highest bidder but to the better armed. The boardroom battle was not a figure of speech. The ownership of major industries such as aluminium was decided by shootouts and assassinations. Entire towns are still owned by gangsters who run the local industry, police and courts.

Times had changed from when Misha was locked in the bowels of the Lenin Library to read *BusinessWeek*. We had a gig at the graduate business school of Moscow University: a big, airy auditorium with a hundred students in pressed jeans and clean trainers and neat haircuts eager to take notes. For the first time there were women in the audience. They all spoke English, which was good and bad

★

– it was not as disjointed as with consecutive translation, but I had to talk for twice as long. I hoped I could think of enough to say. More troubling was that I wasn't sure what level to pitch it at. These kids grew up under Communism, what did they know? What did they teach in a Russian business school? My MBA was about how to be a middle manager in an American multinational. Was it the same here?

They sat through my talk politely, although not many took notes. Obviously my advice on international cross-cultural management was over their heads. I guessed from their diffident questions that they were not sure how to deal with a real live Western international banker-entrepreneur. At the samovar afterwards I made an effort to be affable without being patronizing.

"So what do you want to do when you graduate?" I asked a shy-looking, fresh-faced young lad.

"Mmm, I am trying to buy a company in Britain. It's better than setting up something from scratch, don't you think?"

"Er, how are you going to do this?"

"Mmm, perhaps I shall buy a company on the London Stock Exchange."

"Just like that?"

"Why not. It is a free market, no?"

"Not exactly free. You need money." I tried to let him down gently.

"I have money."

"You need quite a lot of money."

"I have two million dollars."

★

"What?"

"Mmm, I import computer parts from Taiwan and assemble them here. I have a workshop with twenty people."

"Er, I'd be happy to help. I'll give you my card."

"It's OK. I am talking to Kleinworts."

I was stunned. My cup shook under the samovar.

"He has computers, I have mobile phones," said a suave, dark-haired southerner. "It's a bad idea to invest abroad. The returns are so much better here. You can put up a mast for a thousand dollars."

"Ah, but the risk is greater," I said, struggling to play the part of Western know-all.

"My company is offshore in Cyprus. It's safe enough. Price Waterhouse did it for me."

I looked closely round the room. The jeans were designer, the shirts silk, the sweaters cashmere, the Rolexes genuine, the shoes definitely out of my budget.

"Tell me, how many other millionaire entrepreneurs are here?"

The fresh-faced lad looked round. "Mmm, I can see four. Most us have our own businesses."

"Why are you here?"

"To practise our English. You have nothing new to tell us."

"Oh, thanks. I mean at business school."

"We must learn to do business properly, in the right way."

The eldest was 24. They were in computers, building materials, mobile phones, pirate Nintendo games, Doc

Martens shoes, high-value chemicals. They came from well-connected middle-class families, otherwise they would not have got into a prestigious school. Their parents were scientists and diplomats and engineers and administrators, whose world collapsed with the USSR. It embarrassed some of them to be supporting their parents, living like Americans, making so much money. *Biznismyen* in Russian means spiv, street trader, black marketeer. They came to the school for respectability.

CBM went on tour to St Petersburg, Yekaterinburg, Nizhny Novgorod, Kiev, Minsk, company towns and isolated cities that until recently were known only by a number. We went by night sleeper whenever possible. It was a pleasant way to travel. The carriages were warm and the bed firm. Put the centre light out and the little yellow reading lamps made candlelight. A smuggled bottle of vodka, forbidden to take on board, a couple of bottles of cola and the essential Russian accessory for any train journey, a roast chicken. Misha bought me Russian citizens' tickets, which were cheaper than foreigners', so I was under strict instructions to say nothing and act drunk until we were safely locked in our compartment.

"But I don't mind paying," I said. "It's not much."

"*Znachet*, we have our principles," said Misha, deadpan. "And we are working for the good of Russia."

"But what if we get caught?"

Oleg tapped the carton of Marlboros in his bag. He gave the cigarettes to the attendant anyway, which ensured that we had extra pillows, a constant supply of fresh tea and a blind eye to the vodka.

As instructed, I sat catatonically through the preliminaries: checking the tickets, paying for the bedding, sipping tea brought in tall glasses and filigreed metal holders. I peered through the window as the train got under way through desolate cityscapes, with snowflakes swarming in circles round the white street lights and battering like moths at windows of yellow light in the buildings. Soon we were in the endless Russian birch forest, white trunks and branches startled in our light.

Every train had its own character. To St Petersburg they left every half an hour starting at ten with the most luxurious, the Red Arrow, and ending at two with the cheapest and most uncomfortable. In the early trains the first-class compartments converted into two single beds with clean sheets and blankets and had young, efficient attendants ready at any hour to serve piping-hot tea from their electric samovar. The compartments in the last train had four bunks, rags for bedding, as often as not no heating, all the light bulbs except one broken or stolen, and old slags for attendants who spent the journey huddled over an oil stove in their cubicle guarding the precious inventory of tea. The passengers were different, too. After midnight they were down-at-heel with patched felt boots and luggage made of old blankets and string. On the early trains the men were fat and sleek with camel overcoats slung around their shoulders and the women were dressed in fur from head to toe. Their luggage would not have been out of place on the carousels at Zurich and Cannes. Among them were exquisitely beautiful young women on the arms of sheepish foreign men spending their per diems on per noctems with *valutnaya*, foreign-currency whores.

Our lectures were alleviated by hasty tourism, a whirl of onion domes and icons, museums and palaces and galleries and metro stations, vast halls of gilded fixtures and fittings. I preferred writers' house museums, in the irrational hope that genius might rub off. Pushkin's razor, Dostoevsky's hat, Pasternak's pipe, Chekhov's foot warmer, Tolstoy's eiderdown, Bulgakov's graffitied walls, Gogol's wash basin, Yevtushenko's bootscraper, Gorky's pen – all are jumbled together in the bric-a-brac of memory with stuff I can no longer attribute: a vulgar staircase, a truckle bed, a stuffed bear holding out a tray for visiting cards.

The evenings melt into a mishmash of skipping ballerinas, jigging puppets, singing *boyars*, tumbling midgets, clod-hopping bears. I stocked up with *matrioshka* nested dolls and lacquer boxes, painted eggs and spoons that when you get home you don't know what to do with, except keep them away from food and children in case the paint is poisonous. But tourism seemed irrelevant compared with the history that was being made outside the museums.

I sell sea shells

When I was 16 I had recurrent nightmares about a mushroom cloud on a crimson horizon. The dread of nuclear annihilation pervaded our lives. In 1962 our fear focused on the Cuban missile crisis, when JFK's navy blockaded Khrushchev's ships delivering missiles to Castro's Cuba. For twenty-four hours we lived under the real threat of a worldwide nuclear war. On that night I first got tipsy on beer. Bitter, fizzy, intoxicating not so much with alcohol but with excitement, a self-induced euphoria mixed with the fear of imminent death. So when ICBM was invited to give a lecture followed by a sauna at a satellite research institute on a missile base, the prospect of infiltrating Russia's defence system was irresistible.

On a crisp autumn day we took the Dmitrov motorway north for about 100 miles. We were met at a checkpoint and escorted down side roads to an unmarked, rusty gate with an unobtrusive sentry box. There were three more checkpoints on the way in. At the third, our documents were taken away and ten minutes later brought back by a senior officer with brass pips on his greatcoat and a gold badge on his red cap band. He held up my passport and asked me to get out of the

★

car. A spectrum of fates flashed through my mind, from an intimate body search to a stint in the Gulag.

"You are the first foreigner I have seen here," he said. "Welcome." We solemnly shook hands.

The road was lined with blank billboards, so we caught only glimpses of autumnal trees. Underground silos were scattered through the forest, but there was no sign of the missiles that had terrorized my youth. One man was allowed into the forest, a holy man called Grigori. He wore furs and had long black hair and a long black beard and lived in a hut. The guards knew him and left him alone. He might have tried to ride a rocket on its last journey, perched on the point and flying up to heaven. Would he have thought God had finally sent for him? There is not much to cling to on a nose cone, so he would have fallen off into the inferno of the launch pad.

The bunker where we did our turn was a dismal place, unlined concrete and unshaded neon, a pedestrian underpass. All of the audience had at least one PhD and many had two or three. They listened with barely concealed intolerance to my unscientific theories on cultural difference and then asked questions about technical licensing agreements with Japan and the US. When it was clear that I didn't have the wherewithal even to bullshit, they filed out in small groups. Only one stayed to the end, a round little man, even littler if he took off his high-heeled Chelsea boots. He looked in his late 40s, although he could have been younger. Thanks to climate, poor diet, cigarettes, cheap vodka and insecurity, Russian male life expectancy is in the upper 50s, fifteen years less than in the rest of Europe. They age to match. A grey sweatshirt with a Juventus monogram was at odds with this man's unhealthy pallor. His brow was permanently puckered. Every few minutes his scalp twitched and his forehead cleared for an instant, as if he was trying to make his ears go back, like a dog pleading for love. This made his eyes slant and for a split second he had the face of a Tatar. His name was Andrei Denisovich. He waited until Misha and Oleg were busy packing up the projector and took me to one side.

"I have something to sell," he whispered and looked over his shoulder at the door. My heart leapt. A rocket guidance system? A solar radiation drive? How would I smuggle it out? How do you sell things to the Pentagon? This must be a trap. I am underground in one of the world's biggest rocket research complexes. The cameras and microphones must be straining to hear what I think, let alone say. Andrei stood on the balls of his feet and I bent to meet him halfway.

"I have pantacrene." His eyes opened wide and blinked twice. This had to be a code. Or an embarrassing disease.

"Pantacrene?"

"Yessss."

"What do I do with a pantacrene?"

His eyes opened wider. I was definitely an ignoramus. "Like ginseng. From the horns of baby mountain deer. From Mongolia. Guarantee top quality."

My friend Paul markets seal oil from pups clubbed to death in Canada. Baby mountain deer would be an even harder sell.

"Have you got anything more... technological?"

"We have licence for Barents Sea."

Where was the Barents Sea? I had a hazy idea it was off Siberia somewhere. "Who is we? This institute?"

"They have nothing no more. Our group."

A group like ICBM? A couple of chaps in a bedroom struggling to make a living while the world collapsed? "Ah, very good. Oil?"

"Sea shells."

He studied my face for signs of enthusiasm. I let the silence ride, Russian fashion. I hope he mistook my poker face for serious consideration and not the suppression of a giggle.

"It is the part we call White Sea. It is very shallow. The sea shells are ten metres thick. It will take fifty years to dredge them. We can ship direct through Norway. No problem."

Not Siberia, then. "Don't the Norwegians have their own sea shells?"

"Everybody love sea shells."

I cranked up a penetrating stare. A penny dropped. Our budgie gnawed a cuttlefish bone. "Chicken feed?"

"Wonderful cement. In Germany they love the sea-shell cement. All we need is dredger."

"So why do you need me?"

"The financing. Ten thousand dollars downpayment."

"Have you done a feasibility study?"

Old banking habits die hard. When you ask for a feasi-bility study it means you are not interested. If the other party produces a feasibility study, you ask for a business plan. If they produce a business plan, the kiss of death is an environmental impact study.

"One thousand dollars for study. We make joint venture and split fifty-fifty."

So that was it. He wanted five hundred bucks. A night out in London; more than a year's salary for him.

"Feasibility first. Money after."

I had many proposals over the next few months: hydrofoils from Nizhny Novgorod; semi-tanned reindeer hides from Archangelsk; machines to make bricks out of sewage and dog biscuits out of chicken shit from Saratov; a ceramic pipe through which you sucked up sewage and it came out pure water from Kiev. So many entrepreneurial opportunities. So many interesting places to go. I desperately wanted to be part of it.

When you live in an asylum you join in the madness

I went back to London determined to return to Russia. I hoped to make some money, but the main reason was it was so interesting. It was a country remaking itself. It would be exciting to be part of it. I liked the Russians I met and wanted to know them better. They were full of contradictions: hospitable and xenophobic, open and introverted, funny about themselves and prickly when criticized, good-humoured and morose, courageous and vacillating, stubborn and capricious, cruel and sentimental, idealistic and cynical. These were the clichés I came back with, but I wanted to find out what the people were really like.

A franchised baked potato restaurant was the best idea I could come up with. Misha said he would try to locate a Russian partner. It was my job to find a British collaborator and seed financing.

My favourite baked potato takeaway was Jackets next to Brixton Underground station in South London. It was not an obvious choice of joint-venture partner, as I assumed that there was only one branch and if the company was about to broaden its horizons I thought there were more obvious parts of the world to tackle, like the neighbouring communities of Stockwell and Norwood. But I looked it up in the phone book and found that it was technically a chain by virtue of two other outlets in Clapham, a more fashionable part of South London. Malcolm, the chairman and chief executive, plummeted in my esteem when he invited me to come and discuss the idea at his national headquarters above the Clapham High Street restaurant. Didn't he have anything better to do?

I cycled over to Clapham wondering what sort of person owned three fast-food restaurants in South London. I decided middle-class, third-generation black, ex-sportsman, savings invested in a comfortable business. Writer's intuition. He was a whitey in his mid-30s with a posh accent and a tie-dyed T-shirt, jeans and deck shoes without socks. Contagiously cheerful, Malcolm listened to my idea without flinching.

"Sounds good to me," he said, thereby enrolling himself for ever in my list of great blokes.

After a smart public-school education and a degree in politics, Malcolm had a nurture-or-nature career choice. His father had been an important person at Lloyd's of London, the British reinsurance market funded by wealthy investors with unlimited liability. The collapse of Lloyd's in the early 1990s was not yet a twinkle in the eye of destiny and Malcolm could have slipped effortlessly into insurance

★

and a fat City life. But the siren song of long-distance truck driving warbled in his ear and he opted for life on the open motorway. Within a decade Lloyd's Names were ten a penny in minicabbing and painting and decorating, but before the social levelling of mass bankruptcy they were few and far between at drivers' caffs. Between trucking jobs Malcolm squeezed in a few days' photo-stalking stag in the Highlands or pottering about the family retreat in Oxfordshire, which I am sure added variety to talk of coarse fishing and football round the Formica tables of the knights of the road. A preference for baked potatoes over chips would also have set him apart. But none of his eccentricities would have alienated him from his fellow truckers – I have never met anyone easier to get along with and less infected with prejudice or snobbery.

Malcolm got married, but trucking is detrimental to domestic life and he looked for something else to do that would keep him out of the City. It was the beginning of the fast-food explosion. He saw a potato-sized gap in the market between industrial meat hamburgers and processed cheese pizza and launched the first Jackets outlet in Clapham High Street. We passed many happy times over a beer or a bottle of wine rehashing stories of those early days. The search for the perfect potato, the ideal spork (a hybrid of spoon and fork) and the right container for keeping the takeaway hot were sagas of setback and success.

For ten years he was meticulous in pursuit of the quality product and service on which the concept of Jackets is based. Everything is cooked from scratch. There may be a can of kidney beans or tomatoes in the recipes, but the meat comes from the butcher next door and the vegetables from the market. He laboured into the small hours over hot filling recipes, considered diversification into rice 'n' peas and croissants, and struggled with his conscience about hamburgers and fries. He learned to repair the ovens, service the cook-chill cabinets, debug the payroll system. Through determination and flair and a talent for motivating people, the business prospered and Clapham High Street was followed by Clapham Junction and the flagship outlet in Brixton.

I am impressed by anyone who has the energy and vision and guts to start a business from scratch. What I most envy is the ability to apply oneself to the same things day after day. It is an inspiring lesson for any entrepreneur, in Britain or in Russia.

So we shook hands on our partnership. Jackets would be technical adviser to the project in return for an unspecified fee and an unspecified share of the profits. Malcolm had just finished the renovation of the top floor of his building. While he waited for paying tenants, I set up the Russia office. I put up a picture of St Basil's and an aluminium bust of Lenin with his face to the wall.

What made me cycle over more often than I needed was the aroma wafting up the stairs from the kitchen. On a ground bass of baking potato were melodies of frying onions and garlic, stewing tomatoes, herbs, spices, curries, coffee, alternately crescendo and diminuendo. The potato symphony was as lovely as baking bread and it was rare that

★

I could hold out any later than noon before going down-stairs for my first jacket of the day.

On a more professional level, it was convenient to have the technical expertise literally under my feet. After forty minutes in the oven the potatoes were put in the warm cab-inet. If they weren't sold within twenty minutes, Malcolm kept up the quality by throwing them away. A baked potato that is overcooked or let stand too long or, horror of hor-rors, allowed to get cold becomes dry and waxy, its buttery texture and fragrant perfume and subtle taste congealed into putty, its skin bitter and leathery. Microwaving makes them worse. Since my time at Jackets I shudder at the cold brown turds piled in the corner of counters in sandwich bars and cafeterias.

One thing still puzzled me. Malcolm was so practical and level-headed and hands-on. He had his hands full with managing three restaurants and planning expansion into a new shopping centre in Wimbledon. Why on earth did he want to get involved in Russia? The answer was nepotism. His uncle had been a diplomat, the last Governor of Aden, and had ended his career as Australian High Commis-sioner. He had also been a gentleman scholar of Russian, specializing in the national poet Pushkin, and had married a Russian princess from an old St Petersburg family. Malcolm showed me his uncle's translation of *The Bronze Horseman*, probably Pushkin's most famous poem, about the statue of Peter the Great in St Petersburg.

Malcolm's uncle and aunt were dead. There was some-thing touching about rekindling the family's Russian connection. Wouldn't it be romantic and fitting to open up a Jackets in the shadow of the Bronze Horseman? I promised him we would visit St Petersburg at the first opportunity.

The Know-How Fund was an obvious source of finance for our initial development. It was set up by the Foreign Office to fund technical assistance to the former socialist countries of Europe. Having cut my business teeth in an American bank, one of whose dictums was "nothing good ever came out of government", I dreaded the stultifying bureaucracy and blinkered pedestrianism of the petty functionaries who doubtless administered the fund.

In fact they were brilliant. Imaginative, supportive, helpful, fast-moving, they helped us fill out the forms. We had the offer in a week.

Misha phoned from Geneva with news of a possible Russian partner. He was at a conference where he had met the head of the new Farmers' Union, who saw an opportunity for his members to sell their produce at a premium.

I spent Saturday making a video of Jackets and working up a proposal to present in Geneva first thing on Monday morning. Misha phoned again to ask me to bring half a dozen policeman's helmets, cardboard replicas from a souvenir shop would do. I assumed they were give-aways for the presentation.

I flew to Geneva on Sunday and arrived in time for a barbecue at the house of one of the members of the Permanent Trade Mission. There were about fifty people there, all from the Russian international community. Many were in the cast of Gilbert and Sullivan's *Trial by Jury*, which they were going to perform before the Geneva Light Opera Society the following weekend. It was a favourite of Russian amateur choirs. There was a dress rehearsal after lunch and the helmets I brought were props. Choosing between burgers and sausages, the guests broke into "A nice dilemma we have here" and "Never, never, never, since I joined the human race" in English and then Russian and then both together.

Back in London my family stroked their chins and tapped the sides of their noses when I told them. Yeah, *Trial by Jury*. Russians in wigs and bobby helmets. Pull the other one. But you couldn't make it up and if you did, you'd edit it out in the second draft. It was a good introduction to the Gilbertian topsy-turvy I was letting myself in for.

The Jilted Bride was sung by a pretty interpreter. She was barefoot and naked but for a piece of yellow gauze wrapped round herself and tucked under the armpits. Her black hair was fashionably cropped and her eyes were very green. She gave me a chicken wing and I told her about our project.

"Why do you concern yourself with such small things? Do you care so much about what we eat?"

I don't know if I was more troubled by her question or her wicked half-smile. "When you live in an asylum you join in the madness."

"Is that a quotation?"

"If I say it again it will be."

"Do you really care about potatoes?"

"There's a Big World, in which there are big people and big things. And there's a Little World for little people and little things. In the Big World they founded the United Nations, wrote *Dead Souls*, went to the moon. In the Little World they made Barbie dolls, composed the Chicken Dance, invented the trouser press. In the Big World people try to make man more noble. In the Little World people try to put food on the table."

"That is a quotation. Ilf and Petrov. *The Twelve Chairs*?"

"*The Little Golden Calf.*"

"You didn't say if you cared about potatoes."

"Do you know the expression 'meal ticket'? What do you care about?"

"The future of Russian democracy."

"Ah. This is nice chicken."

The Usher came to tell us it was time for the rehearsal. The Jilted Bride went away and I could stop pulling my stomach in. While they got changed, I set up my video on the television in the living room. It was a good opportunity to test the Jackets concept on a Russian focus group and fortuitously they were dressed up as judge and jury, with gowns, wigs and helmets. I should have started my pitch with the Defendant's "Oh, gentlemen, listen, I pray", but since I burbled in the chorus when we did it at school I have forgotten it.

The first thing they noticed was that the staff of Jackets and half the customers were black.

"Is this African food? Russians do not like Africans," said the Foreman of the Jury.

"But this Johnston is white. Why does he not hire white people?" asked the Learned Judge, taking up the theme.

"Is this Kleppem in the ghetto?" asked the First Bridesmaid.

"They aren't African. They are as British as I am. In England we aren't prejudiced," I said, wishing fervently it were true.

The jury argued whether to Russians a potato is as aspirational as a Quarter Pounder. With an album of promo photos I tried to convince them that our customers would not associate our symmetrical, smooth-skinned delicacies with the knobbly, leathery mutants they found in the markets of Moscow. Fortunately, someone mentioned Idaho and the American connection appeased the doubters. The clincher came at the end of my video, a shot of the street outside. Two doors away from Jackets was a new McDonald's, a cross for Malcolm to bear, but now and for the months to come our main credential. We were in the same street, therefore in the same league, as the Golden Arches.

It was unrealistic for me to wish for a closing chorus of "Joy unbounded, with wealth surrounded", but I had hoped for a little more enthusiasm. I am deeply ashamed to say that we edited the video that night to give a misleading impression of the ethnic diversity of South London. And we gave almost as much screen time to McDonald's as to Jackets.

On Monday morning we reported to the Russian Mission on Avenue de la Paix. The place was buzzing as weighty matters from the Big World were being discussed at the United Nations. Important and serious men, some in uniform, paced the corridors with shiny portfolios. We had use of a meeting room for an hour before it was given over to preparing for negotiations in the Palais des Nations. The technician who set up the video machine assured us that it was secure and that the walls were soundproof and swept daily for bugs. It was thrilling to be at the centre of world events. We were proud to make a contribution to peace through the development of free and democratic markets in the former Soviet Union and commercial cooperation between formerly antagonistic global powers. And would you like extra cheese with that?

While we waited, Misha briefed me again on the Farmers' Union. In the liberalization of 1992, millions of roubles had been allocated from the national budget for the encouragement of private farms. Collective farms were obliged to hive off 10 per cent of their land to private individuals. Farmers received a capital grant and annual loans. The Farmers' Union was set up to represent them and distribute the largesse. A top-down state bureaucratic institution, its independence derived not from its members but from its rivalry with the Ministry of Agriculture, which was run by die-hard believers in the state collective system.

The Farmers' Union director was a distinguished professor of economics and a member of the Economic Commission of the recently defunct Council for Economic Planning, Gosplan. Since 1921 Gosplan had produced the Soviet Union's five-year plans. I hoped he was not too much of a big-picture chap to appreciate the subtleties of the takeaway trade.

As befitted a professor he arrived fifteen minutes late. He was tall and white-haired, with the slight stoop that tall people affect, but his face did not fit. It was young and wrinkle free, as if he were being played by a student. I took to him immediately.

He came with four hangers-on, whose cards announced various complicated job titles in the Ministry of Agriculture and the Trade Mission, but their clothes looked too sharp for Min of Ag types. I never saw or heard of them again and they may have been minders from the Embassy. The New Russia was only three years old and habits die hard. I studied their cards not so much to divine their status but to learn their names and patronymics, by which we addressed each other for the rest of the meeting; except that I, to my disappointment, remained Mister Mole and not John Genrivitch.

We all shook hands and stared stony faced at one another as we muttered *orchen priadna*, pleased to meet you. It is thought inane to smile on first meeting. They sat down in a solemn row, hands folded across their stomachs. I knew not to start my dog-and-pony with a joke as I would with Americans, as this is considered boorish. They were stock still and expressionless through the video and my cogent analysis of why the project would be good for farmers, consumers and international peace. I made much of the support from the British government through the Know-How Fund. The clincher was that a modest restaurant with fifty seats would need 100 tons of potatoes, 30 tons of dairy products and 10 tons of meat a year. In the UK to get 100 tons of acceptable bakers you needed to grow 400 tons. Many small farms would be required to supply us.

When I finished, the men from the Farmers' Union stood up and made for the door. The professor shook hands last.

"Hmmm. This is impossible in present conditions. Our farmers are not prepared. We do not have the infrastructure. We do not have the legal framework for franchising. You cannot find premises like this in Moscow. We do not have the finance for the business or the farmers. All the equipment would have to be imported at very great cost. The difficulties are insurmountable. Hmmm."

Misha closed the door and we locked in a comradely embrace.

"Yesss! He bought it."

Sure enough, the professor phoned Misha from the airport that evening. We should go to Moscow at our earliest convenience and discuss "a possible cooperation".

This is Russia, Mister John

I was given a desk on the fourth floor of the Farmers' Union headquarters. Having braved the ferocious doorkeepers, short and round Mother Russias in knitted tea-cosy hats, you were bathed in the atmosphere of bureaucracy, a semi-solid gas of recycled superheated air, sweet tobacco, acrid disinfectant, eggy effluvium, paper and body odour. I shared the office with Afanasy, who was to be the Jackets project coordinator, and Natasha, our assistant and interpreter.

Afanasy was in his 50s. He was bald, tanned and wore gold-rimmed glasses and the kind of spivvish grey suits with broad pinstripes affected by louche Tory MPs. Despite his urbane appearance, his passion was fishing. Many years before he had been attached to the Russian delegation to the UN and spoke English with a thick Brighton Beach accent. He was so good at coordinating the project that he had coordinated it all away to other people. At every question I asked he shook his head.

"Jarn, I am only de coordinator. By no means. You gotta ask somebody else…" *By no means* was a verbal tic like Misha's *znachet*.

Natasha was in her late 20s. She came to work dressed for cocktail parties in shimmering dresses with gossamer sleeves and sparkly high heels, or for left-wing dinner parties in shawls and layers of ethnic skirts. She spent the first half hour of the day cross-legged on her chair in meditation, hands down on the desk. I asked if she was a Buddhist. Astralist, she said. I didn't take it further in case an involuntary smirk blighted our relationship.

My first task was to identify suppliers of raw materials. I caused consternation when I suggested we should visit some farmers to find out at first hand what they could supply and what support they needed. Many practical difficulties were put in my way,

"By no means. Dere's no point. Dey don't know whadday need," rasped Afanasy.

"How do we know this if we don't ask them?"

"Jarn, I know farmers," he said, carefully inserting a Dunhill into an amber cigarette holder. "Dey don' unnerstand."

"So what do we base our plan on?"

"Regional directors will make reports."

"I'd rather see for myself."

"You waste your time. By no means. Dey give you false information to screw more money outa de Union. Dese peasants are money-grubbin' sons-o-bitches. Stay away from 'em."

"The farms are in countryside," revealed Natasha, as if this were an affront to nature. "How will you find them? How will you get to them? Dzhorn, it is not practical."

I scoured the dictionary for the meanings of the grace words *Jarn* and *Dzhorn* until I twigged they were my name.

I asked the advice of Flor Ivanovitch, the director of the research department. He was a round-faced young man with pale-blue eyes, thinning fair hair and a penchant for mustard – mustard tweed jacket, mustard trousers, mustard shirt, mustard tie. He also thought that field research was an odd thing to do. He gave me more reasons it would be difficult.

"John, we are embarrassed to let a foreigner see conditions in countryside. And they are frightened you will hear bad things about the Union."

"But the Union is the farmers' organization. We represent them. We serve their interests."

"Theoretically this is true. Unfortunately, most of the people in this building are seconded from the Ministry of Agriculture. They have spent their whole lives fighting farmers. They hate the countryside."

"Don't they go to *dachas* at the weekend?"

"*Dachniks* look down on country people. Uncultured, they say, and dishonest. And the country people resent the *dachniks* because they have money and cars and are arrogant."

"Jeez, Flor. How am I supposed to get things done?"

"This is Russia, Mister John."

I did what you do in Russia to get things done – I went straight to the top man. After hanging round the professor's anteroom for an hour or so, chatting up his secretary and watching a Mexican soap with her, I was summoned in. The corner office was light and airy with windows on two sides and blond-wood panelling. It was dominated by a massive desk heaped with books and papers. Another table held a computer and two televisions. Two brown leather sofas at right angles were for visitors. The host's leather throne was in front of them. The rest of the office was cluttered with agricultural gifts and souvenirs.

The nerve centre and the real sign of the professor's status was a row of six telephones, all different colours. They weren't just for show; this is how a Russian chief executive runs his empire. "He has the power of the telephone" doesn't mean he has a telephone that always works, although that is already a sign of superior status. It means he can pick it up and give an order and the person on the other end will carry it out. That is a sign of real power.

I had five minutes to make my petition. He thought it was a novel idea, but he picked up the phone and with one call to Afanasy it was arranged. Afanasy swallowed his misgivings with good grace and found the closest farmer to Moscow who would be willing to suffer the intrusion of a foreigner.

In Russia it is eccentric to do anything on your own. For business you must travel in a delegation, for leisure you must travel in a group. So Afanasy, Natasha and two other men I had never met climbed into a bright yellow minibus one damp Monday morning. We were in holiday mood, the novelty of our mission and the break from the tedium of a day in the office infecting even Afanasy with cheerfulness.

Our driver, Igor, wore a tweed overcoat, long scarf, gauntlets and a leather hunting hat with the untied earflaps dangling. I feared for the heating in the minibus, but I needn't have worried. He must have learned his driving behind a tractor and this was his uniform. He complained that the bus was foreign junk, made in Latvia, and that they ought to have given us a decent Russian one. I made the mistake of taking him seriously until he grinned. Russian humour can be as deadpan as English. Latvia had been independent for only two years and Russian troops were still on its soil.

We took the Leningrad motorway out of town and after an hour or so turned onto a potholed asphalt road. For another two hours we jolted in the drizzle through uninterrupted forest. Apart from a few tractors and trailers and a long truck loaded with logs, there was no traffic. An occasional pedestrian plodded along with a shopping bag. Where on earth were they going? We were in the middle of nowhere. The asphalt stopped at a junction in a clearing with a choice of three dirt roads. There were no signs or landmarks and Igor had no map, but he confidently chose the one least travelled. When Afanasy asked him if he was sure, he tapped the side of his lumpy nose. The road was sandy mud and the side windows were soon stuccoed, but it was less bumpy.

What we could see of the colours outside was exquisite. Russian forests are not just row after row of birches, but vast arboretums of different trees. Not that I can tell you what they were. My arboreal education stopped in the school cadet force with the pines and bushy-topped trees we were taught to use as landmarks when aiming our antiquated rifles.

We had a closer acquaintance with the bushy tops when the engine coughed into silence and the smell of petrol filled the bus. We got out. The glistening road ran straight to vanishing points in either direction. There was nothing to be heard but whispering leaves and pattering rain and the creaking of the cooling engine and Igor cursing all Latvians and their mothers as he tinkered under the bonnet. The rest of us huddled under a tree and smoked in silence, city dwellers cowed by the immensity of nature and the prospect of a long, wet walk. Coming from England, where the countryside is suburbia spread thin, the vast emptiness was unnerving. And this was only 100 miles from Moscow. It was inconceivable that there should be any other human being, let alone habitation, within 50 miles.

"Trouble, comrades?" asked a man in the trees behind us. We started as one and spun round to see a man in the Russian version of a Barbour outfit, brown oilskins and khaki bush hat. He was in his 50s with a grainy outdoorsman's face and a thick black moustache. A shotgun lolling in the crook of his elbow and a bulging game bag, with a russet wing and a furry paw peeping from under the flap, established his credentials. He strolled to the back of the bus where Igor was unloading the brimming toolbox without which no Russian driver leaves home.

Igor took out a pile of empty fertilizer bags and laid them on the mud under the bus. He lay down on his back and inched his way underneath with a pair of pliers and some wire.

"Fuel line bust," he said. "It drips petrol but I don't think we've lost much."

"Shall I hold your cigarette for you, brother?" asked the hunter. Igor handed it to him and he stubbed it out in the mud.

We introduced ourselves. His name was Ivan and he was by profession a steeplejack, a word out of reach of their English and my Russian, but by way of mime we got there in the end via tree surgeon, mountaineer and helicopter pilot. He had a *dacha* nearby. He quizzed me about steeplejacking in England. I was eloquent about the population of steeplejacks, their pay and conditions, their climbing techniques, the ratio of new build to demolition and so on. I made it all up, but when foreigners take an interest it seems churlish to say you haven't the foggiest. In return I asked him about the rural economy in the area and he probably made up his answers too. The natural desire to please accounts for much of the misinformation in feasibility studies and travel books, doubtless including this one. When I asked him what he thought of the political situation and the economy, he shrugged.

"We live in our Russia. They live in theirs," he said.

Igor emerged from under the bus, donned his gauntlets and, after some dry coughs from him and the engine, both lit up and we were on our way. Ivan came with us, his aura of cordite and wet leaves adding to the fug of cigarette smoke and body odour we had been fermenting since Moscow.

He took us back to the crossroads with the asphalt road and after half an hour or so we broke out of the trees into a flat, grassy plain. The mud changed from sandy to black. Ivan said it had belonged to the *kolkhoz*, the state collective farm, until they were obliged to hand it over to private farmers two years before. Afanasy said they were probably glad to get rid of it.

Ivan got out here, where he had parked his truck. We wished each other well with much handshaking and fraternal greetings to the steeplejacks of England, which I take this opportunity to pass on.

We passed a field where two women poked around in the mud. Although a novice to farming, I recognized a heap of little brown potatoes. There was no cart or vehicle or other mechanical aid in sight. Ahead we saw a house and its outbuildings and the tracery of a fence silhouetted against a vast, lowering sky. By now the track was a river of thin slush about a foot deep. Through the gate in the fence it widened into a lake of thicker mud, which was the farmyard.

Igor knew he should not stop. He changed down and revved the engine and headed for a shed where two men were working on the roof with a welding machine. We fishtailed towards the incandescent blue light of the welder, a beacon in the sludge that covered the windscreen. We slithered, stalled and stuck fast in the morass.

Afanasy opened the sliding door. We were twenty yards away from solid ground. The mud came up to the sill. A pig

⭐

swam away like a dolphin, arching and plunging, arching and plunging. One of the men on the roof climbed down and waded towards us, the mud up to the knees of his tall rubber boots. Short and beefy with bandy legs and bandy arms, he wore a short leather jacket and a matching Lenin cap the colour of the mud, a true son of the soil.

While Igor flogged the starter motor we crowded in the doorway to make our introductions. Our host's name was Vasily. His round, pink, featureless face was enlivened by startling blue eyes.

My banker's suit and Clarks brogues were certainly no match for the conditions. I feared I might have to be carried piggyback to the shore, a piquant introduction to my official duties as international consultant to the Union. Vasily said he had a spare pair of boots that we could take it in turns to use.

Meanwhile, Igor got the engine going and gunned it alternately in third and reverse, digging us deeper in a fountain of mud. Then Vasily had the idea of us all playing sardines in the back over the drive wheel to increase the purchase. It worked. In clouds of smoke and mud we slithered to the edge of the viscous lake and solid ground.

It stopped raining. The sky was lightening and the breeze turned from humid to crisp. In the flickering glare of the welder I made a tour of inspection, venturing as far as was amenable to my leather uppers, skipping over cowpats and pigpats and casting a townie's eye over the establishment. The house had two storeys and a pitched roof and was made entirely of wood. It looked American, except that the wood was genuine and not metal siding. The outbuildings had a more Irish feel, ramshackle huts made of anything that came to hand: wood, brick, breeze block, corrugated iron. The welders were making a steel frame for another shed out of girders strong enough for a bomb shelter.

Half a dozen cows shuffled in a pen made of stakes and branches. A dozen little piglets ran out of the barn, squealed and snuffled and ran back in again. We followed them. In one corner on a wooden pallet were a milking stool, metal buckets and metal milk churns that in Britain you only see now on model railways. In another corner, protected from the pigs by wire mesh, was a heap of potatoes, little brown knobbly things. There was not much else to see. A trailer, a plough-looking thing, a beat-up Niva. It all seemed very primitive. Was this the future of Russian agriculture? It felt more like the past.

Vasily invited us into the house and we sat round the kitchen table. He apologized that his wife and daughter weren't here to wait on us. They were the women we had seen picking potatoes. He took out of the fridge a bottle of vodka, a cucumber and a plate of pickled piglet tails, which are tastier than they sound and a lot tastier than they look. He had been a brigadier at the *kolkhoz*, in charge of a brigade of fifty workers. He was full of confidence and authority and had a voice to match. He delivered the most innocuous comment like an order.

"Eat! Drink! Welcome!"

Two years ago Vasily had taken over twenty hectares and had just negotiated a lease on another ten. He got a Union grant to build a house and the farm gave him a tractor. I asked if he had a Farmer's Loan from the bank.

"I must give 30 per cent kickback to the bank manager! Borrowing is foolish! Lending is a crime! It is not the Russian way!"

He started with a load of seed potatoes from the *kolkhoz* on extended credit and sold the harvest in the local market at 1000 per cent profit. He used the money to buy cows and pigs and more seeds. But now he could not afford to sell in the market. In the name of privatization city officials leased the market concessions to each other for next to nothing and charged traders exorbitant rents. As for trucking stuff to Moscow, not a hope. The markets were controlled by Chechens.

"Money! Who wants it! The rouble! Bah!"

"How do you pay for your new shed?"

"I give pigs and cream to the *kolkhoz*! They build it for me!"

Vasily was out of the money system. Instead of buying and selling he bartered for everything, from petrol to vodka. It was the Soviet *blat*, managers of enterprises traded commodities and services between themselves. Or the old system of *kolkhozniks* working so many days for the collective and so many days on their own plots. Or the older system of serfs owing so many days to their owner and spending the rest on their private strips. I suspected there was something more in his relationship with his old comrades at the *kolkhoz* than met the eye, but I knew I would never find out. As for our fact-finding mission, the only fact

I could be certain of was that Vasily came far down the list of potential potato suppliers.

Under the pretext of finding the lavatory, I went outside in the hope that a few deep breaths of fresh air would keep the piglet tails down. The welder was still busy, strobing the yard with sparky blue light. Dark clouds overhead made dusk while golden bright sky over the distant forest backlit the countryside. There was a timeless enchantment about it. Half-remembered evocations of Russian landscapes in Turgenev and Gogol and Tolstoy jostled for a hearing. For a moment I was no longer the foreigner in a suit with a briefcase but a guest of the land, calling to me. The soul of Russia was out there. I wanted to get closer to it, away from the buildings and the welding. In the corner where I stood on a rough planking deck were a couple of stepping stones across the mud to firm ground.

I realized my mistake as I was making it, which is more mortifying than being taken by surprise. You may have seen the root of my error in the words "stepping stones". You may already have guessed what they really were. I am not sure what gave me the first clue. It could have been the movement under my feet, the grunt, the pointy ear flicking up or the glinting oxyacetylene eye. When I recreate the scene, which I do as seldom as possible, I am minded of James Bond skipping across the backs of crocodiles. Crocodiles are different from pigs. Their skin is knobbly not slick. They swim flat and do not buck like a bronco.

At that moment Natasha came out to see where I had got to. She was treated to the inauguration of the sport of pig surfing. For one exhilarating moment I rode the mud. Unfortunately I am no more skilful at surfing on a pig than I am on a surf board and the outcome was equally inevitable.

Everyone was very kind. After a hose-down to get the worst off, I went inside for a hot shower. Vasily lent me underwear, a work shirt, dungarees and rubber boots. Everyone clapped when I went back into the kitchen.

"O! *Kolkhoznik*! Welcome to Russia!"

We left before the women came back to give us dinner, piling into the bus and crowding over the drive wheel to ford the farmyard. We passed them still stooping over their potatoes in the gathering dusk. There was no sign of Ivan the steeplejack and rabbits browsed with impunity along the verge. My Russian shirt was as itchy as hell.

Caviar for the particular

Misha went back to his day job in Rome. With typical generosity he lent me his apartment in Moscow. It was about fifteen minutes' walk from a metro station on the Green line going north. The way home was through a street market, across a park, past a cinema and into a development of brick-built apartment blocks. It was a solid middle-class residential area, civil servants, academics and professional people, a couple of rungs below the luxury riverside and hilltop pads of the *nomenklatura* and the new rich.

The ground-floor entrance had an intercom system, long perished, and a lock operated by a number pad. 1812 was the code. The staircase was dirty and badly lit. Cleaning and maintenance were done by the person who couldn't stand it any longer. We went three days without a light bulb, feeling our way in the pitch dark and striking a match to see our keyholes. My neighbour Alexei cracked first. The windows on the half landings were broken and covered in sacking to stop birds coming in. The stone steps were worn with chunks missing in the middle, so it was advisable to hug the wall when going down. The predominant smell was cat shit, as owners kept the litter outside their front doors. There were other smells too: mouldering concrete, tonight's dinners, and cabbage of course – or perhaps drains, they are easily confused.

In Britain, if you buy your own council house, you replace the standard-issue plywood door with nail-studded mahogany, a swirly bull's-eye porthole and wrought-iron fitments. The Russian equivalent is a bullet-proof steel door with reinforced hinges and an array of locks. Misha's door was covered in plastic imitation leather, but the others in our block were raw steel. They were massive things, crudely welded and stained with the cutting torch, but with an attractive shot-silk patina.

Ordinary Russians gasped when I invited them in for the first time. Although they tried not to show it, they were overawed. Glum-faced, as is polite before the first drink, they sat on the white leather sofa in slippered feet and conducted a surreptitious survey.

The standard Russian flat was dark, small and pokey. A kitchen with plain white tiles or distempered walls looked like an English kitchen of the 1940s. Sometimes there was room for two or three people to eat round a small table. Off a corridor were one or two small bedrooms and a living room crammed with furniture. A record player, a television set and these days a computer. The main difference between Russian and British homes lay in the floor-to-ceiling shelves of books in all the rooms and corridors. Every surface was covered in bric-a-brac, ornaments and souvenirs on doilies and mats. The apartments felt stuffed, like the bijou residences of empty nesters when they sell the family house but can't bear to get rid of the junk of decades. On a winter's evening in a snowstorm at 20 below they are wonderfully cosy, but I always felt like I was visiting Granny.

Misha did away with all this. He demolished the walls and made an open-plan living room with a raised dining platform and a galley kitchen behind a divider. The bedroom, bathroom and toilet led straight off the living room. On top of these conveniences under the ceiling were a washing machine and drier, accessible by a handy step ladder. There was a small alcove for a hall, just room enough for two to take off their shoes.

If the layout wasn't revolutionary enough, the furnishings took the breath away, from Russian lungs at least. White leather sofa and armchairs. Smoked-glass dining table with gold legs and matching chairs with red cushions. Crystal chandelier. Spotlights. Italian standard lamp with foot-operated switch that evinced cries of wonder. The bed was a king-size mattress on a carpet-covered platform. Navy-blue sheets. The walls and doors of the fitted wardrobes were covered in mirror tiles. The wall beside the bed was entirely papered with an alpine forest scene. When the sun shone in the morning it was like being in bed on the balcony of a Swiss chalet, bathed in light and icy glitter. At night, with greenish-yellow streetlights irradiating the scene, it became a post-Chernobyl forest, glowing in the dark.

★

"Your friend has connections. Be careful," said Flor from research.

"See how Russians have taste when they get the chance? By no means," said Afanasy.

Women were even more impressed than men.

"This is so international... so elegant... so sophisticated," said Natasha as she stroked the nylon carpeting on the walls.

"Is your apartment in London like this?" asked Olga.

"Oh yes, I have carpet on the ceiling as well. And a transparent armchair with real fish inside it."

I didn't use the kitchen much. My Russian friends were extraordinarily hospitable at their apartments or their *dachas*. If I needed to shop I used the local street market for fresh stuff like fruit and vegetables. Much of it was grown in the seller's allotment or *dacha* and was reasonably priced. The big covered markets were dominated by Caucasians who imported produce from the south. Their stuff was expensive, out of reach of people living on ordinary salaries. The best bread was from the state-owned bakery where you queued up at a hatch for bricks of delicious black bread, which is in fact brown. It had a delicious tang and nuttiness. For the rest I usually went to the supermarket at the Irish House. Sunday breakfast was Irish rashers and listening to the BBC World Service like a true expat – or should it be expaddy?

Out of guilt and parsimoniousness I sometimes shopped in Russian shops, the *gastronom* and the *produkti*, for specialities like sour cream and smoked fish. And for less lovely things like tinned sprats in tomato sauce, known as unmarked graves, a disgusting mess of eyes and bones that I found curiously addictive. But it was such a drag to queue three times, once at the counter to discover the price from a surly assistant, then remember it while you queued at the *kasse* to pay, and finally lining up again at the counter with the receipt to get your shopping.

I did my best to live up to the apartment's sophistication. I got in caviar from a covered market next to the Circus, a half-kilo jam jar, about five dollars' worth, expensive by Russian standards but I always bought the best Beluga. You had to be careful you were not getting counterfeit, but Misha introduced me to a dealer he trusted. I laid in a dozen cases of 1982 Chablis from a kiosk next to Dynamo stadium at an outrageous foreigner's price of a dollar a bottle. At another kiosk I found a dozen boxes of Romeo y Julieta half coronas at three dollars a box. So after a hard day at the potato business I could relax in style, a step up from my usual Happy Hour of a pint of lager, a Hamlet and a packet of pork scratchings.

I found that the caviar went best on black bread, but a couple of spoonfuls on tagliatelle is nice, with a bit of cream, and it goes surprisingly well on a fried egg. A word to the wise: it doesn't go at all with baked beans. Too salty.

It was illegal to take caviar out of the country unless you bought it at the special airport shop at special prices. Bags were X-rayed on departure for little round tins. You got round this by decanting it into sandwich bags and squashing it flat between your shirts. It freezes well, so we stocked up the freezer, except for one shipment that ended up in the Sunlight Shirt Laundry in Camberwell. Alas, all good things…

Over the years the caviar trade tightened up and you had to pay five bucks for a little blue tin. The decent wine got diverted to posh new restaurants and a more visionary entrepreneur than I snapped up Moscow's entire stock of R&Js, which remained unreplenished with the decline of barter trade with Cuba.

I had first tasted Russian caviar in the Time of Stagnation. We were on a package trip to Moscow and St Petersburg, or Leningrad as it was then, in the middle of winter. Traders lurked outside the hotel. In those days it was a risky business, unless they had good connections and paid a percentage of their takings to the police. It also felt risky to be one of their customers. There were stories of Westerners being arrested for changing money and selling jeans. In those days you suspected everything was a trap, but with his open face and lovely smile it was hard to believe that Yuri was working for the KGB. I strolled over the road from the hotel to look at the frozen Neva. He came up beside me. I ignored him. He stared down at the ice like a tourist and not a tout.

"Where are you from?" he asked.

"I have no dollars and no jeans."

"You are very deprived. I have dollars and I have jeans. Do you have caviar?"

"No. No caviar either."

He put a jam jar on top of the wall in front of me. It looked like the blackberry and damson jam my mother used to make, black and viscous, sealed with a circle of greaseproof paper and a rubber band.

"Caviar," he said, "to the general."

"I'm not a general."

"General means the general public, not a military rank. It is Shakespeare. *Hamlet*, if I am not mistaken."

"Are you Russian? How do you know Shakespeare?"

"All Russians know Shakespeare. And Robbie Burns. And Jack London. I have been to English special school. And this is real Beluga. Caviar for the particular."

"I said I have no dollars and no jeans."

"You Westerners are so materialistic. Your civilization will collapse. It is a present from Yuri. Taste it."

He popped off the rubber band and the disc of paper and produced a wooden spoon from an ice-cream tub. He cleaned it on the crust of frozen snow on top of the wall and handed it to me. "Be my guest."

I had eaten caviar before, in Iran, but by the mocha spoonful. I loaded the wooden spoon and licked it off. It was real caviar. It was also true that Yuri didn't want dollars or jeans. He wanted my Y-fronts.

"Have you seen the Russian underwear?" he asked.

"I have not had the pleasure."

"Thick, black and baggy. They itch until they have been washed ten times. Only the kids want jeans. The big guys in town go to their girlfriends in the afternoon, they want to walk round in Y-fronts. Wolsey, yes?"

"How about Marks & Spencer's?"

I was constipated for a fortnight through eating caviar with a dessert spoon at every meal. Which was fortunate, as I had only the one pair of black baggies Yuri threw in with the deal. I washed them every night, but that was OK because the radiators were so hot.

The front door of Misha's building opened onto a square. Later on in winter the trees were bare and it was deserted, except for a huddled figure bustling home, a driver scraping his windows clear, a few dog owners loitering round yellow patches in the snow. There were Alsatians and Dobermans and mongrel guard dogs, second line of defence after the steel doors, but there were also lapdogs, poodles and chihuahuas and dachshunds and ratty crossbreeds, all lovely to their owners but an embarrassment to men on the other end of dainty leads.

When it was warm enough, women in headscarves sat on benches outside the doors to gossip and keep an eye on passers-by. Men tinkered with decrepit cars. Children played on swings and slides in the sandy enclosure. There were garages at one side of the square where furtive young men in black leather jackets and jeans loaded and unloaded sacks and boxes from unmarked vans. Walk too close and they stared at you, blank-faced and threatening.

Apart from Alexei, an old man habitually dressed in a three-piece dark suit and embroidered Siberian socks with whom I shared a landing, I spoke to nobody. The rest of my fellow residents plodded past each other with hardly a grunted greeting. It has been said that this attitude to others – not interacting, not looking, not speaking – was a legacy of Soviet times when strangers were not trusted. I was ignored, never greeted, never challenged, yet I must have stuck out a mile.

Gradually I became less conspicuous. It had nothing to do with physical characteristics. Moscow was an imperial capital and the streets still teemed with exotic physiognomies: tall flat-faced Mongols, creased-eyed Tatars, swarthy Caucasians, every sort of Germanic, Latin, Balkan, Finnish, Uzbek, Kirghiz, Chinese, Japanese.

My first step was to wear a hat. Only Westerners walked around bare-headed on a cold day. I bought a Santa's helper ski hat with a long tassel and a snowflake motif to wear with a long grey padded anorak. The key to anonymity was not so much the clothes as the demeanour. I developed the Moscow trudge, plastic bag in each hand, head down, looking neither right nor left. I knew I had succeeded when people came up to ask directions.

The only person in the square who greeted me was Yefrem, a *bomzhi* or homeless man, who lived in a cubbyhole under the stairs down to the basement area of the block next to mine. He was in his 40s and shaggy. Hair and beard and scarf and fur hat and greatcoat and disgusting boots were all moulting. Beady black eyes and a strawberry nose peeped out from the pelt. Our residents' association paid him a pittance to paint out the graffiti on the estate. There were a dozen blocks of flats and four squares, so there was plenty to do. Graffiti was a new phenomenon, a by-product of *Glasnost* that freed artistic expression. Not only did Russians learn graffiti from the West but they wrote half of it in English.

Yefrem's work gave him an extensive vocabulary that he practised on me. He lay in wait, and when he saw me beetling across the courtyard in the morning and trudging back in the evening, he popped up to greet me.

"Can't buy me love."

"Hello, Yefrem."

"Fook Livairpool."

"Good thinking, Yefrem."

"Make lyorve and vore."

"I'll do my best."

He was a graffiti audiobook for the visually impaired. Why did he recite his phrases to me? Partly to improve his pronunciation. I gave up correcting him because he only repeated the same mistakes over and over again. Partly out of hospitality, to make me feel at home. Partly because he was drunk or crackers or both.

At a rough estimate there are about 50,000 *bomzhi* in Moscow and 4 million in Russia. *Bomzhi* is an acronym for "without fixed place of residence". In English "of no fixed abode" means you don't have an address. In Russian it means much more. Every Russian over the age of 14 has an internal passport, the equivalent of a European identity card. It contains the name, date and place of birth, military service, marital status and names of children under 14. It also carries a registered address, still known as a *propiska*, although the official name was changed to registration in

1991. The *propiska* entitles the holder to education, health services and welfare benefits. In 1998 the Constitutional Court of Russia declared the *propiska* unlawful and Moscow's Mayor Luzhkov declared that he was ignoring it.

Economic migrants, refugees and any outsiders find it very difficult to get a *propiska*, especially if they cannot afford the necessary fees and bribes. You lose it by losing your apartment, moving to another city or going to jail. Repatriation from former Soviet republics and the wars in the Caucasus have created hundreds of thousands of internal refugees without right of work or residence. Once a *bomzhi* it is very difficult to stop being one. A *bomzhi* has neither a home nor the right to one nor any access to emergency shelters, hostels and so on. In Moscow and other places they stretch the rules by giving emergency shelter in winter to people who have lost their *propiska*, but not to those who were never entitled to one. A few charities struggle to help them, but generally they are hounded and despised. Smaller cities like Vladimir solve their *bomzhi* problem by rounding them up and carting them to the municipal rubbish dump, a symbolic as well as practical solution.

Yefrem was lucky. He was a *bomzhi* but he was *our bomzhi*. He had a place to live and a livelihood.

You will not find such a potato in the whole of Russia

The bedrock of our project was that there would be no problem with the supply of raw material in the biggest potato-producing country in the world. Russians eat nearly 20 million tons of potatoes a year.

Mustard Flor from research introduced me to Basil Iurivitch, the president of Russian Potatoes. His office was in the Agriculture Ministry. He had been director of the Soviet Potato Board until it was hived off as a *konzern*, an independent company owned by producers and research centres. Its main function, as in the old days, seemed to be filing and collating the reports that lined his dingy eyrie. With his job Basil held on to his chunky grey-blue suit, Druzhba papiros cigarettes, the picture of Lenin behind the desk.

I outlined the plan. He said he would personally procure as many potatoes as I wanted. Russia had over 180 varieties of potato, so surely one would be perfect for us. He declaimed the names like poetry: Ariadna, Kalinka, Talovsky, Orgonyok.

We smiled at each other across the tea glasses, already basking in mutual profit and success. I handed him a colour photo of a Jackets potato, a perfect Estima, with a smooth, glistening skin, opened like a flower, cradling a succulent sauce of mince and red peppers and kidney beans. He took it in both hands and contemplated the marvel in silence, broken only by the fizzing of his papiros.

"You will not a find such a potato in the whole of Russia," he said.

"But I've seen them. In the market. Lovely stuff."

"They are from Hungary."

McDonald's sourced as much they could from Russia, to the extent of advising and investing in farms. I supposed they had a surplus of potatoes that they would be happy to dispose of at premium prices. I went to see Dave, their technical director, a very pleasant and helpful chap, at their production facility in Solntsevo.

I took Petya, Olga's son, with me. He was deeply shocked that we had to wear white coats and hair nets. He put me on notice that if I wanted him or his friends to work at Jackets they would refuse hair nets. They were Russians. They were men. He calmed down when I said they could wear baseball hats.

I put a deal to Dave. We would buy the biggest and best potatoes from McDonald's at whatever multiple of the market price he wished. It would be a tiny fraction of the amount they used for fries. Dave countered with his deal. He would buy all the potatoes we produced and did not use at whatever multiple of the market price we wished. This

★

was chilling. It meant that not even McDonald's had cracked it. What hope had we got?

The quest for a bakeable potato took me and Natasha fifty miles north of Moscow to the town of Dmitrov. We went in her old Niva, a boxy four-wheel drive. In Russia a 4x4 is actually useful. Off-road does not mean the supermarket car park and the gravel drive. Once you leave the city centre and the motorways, off-road is the same as on-road: snow, mud, ruts and potholes. The Niva was built for utility rather than comfort. But it starts at 30 below and has a road clearance that makes it look permanently jacked up.

We set off after breakfast on a lovely late autumn morning. The road criss-crossed the Moscow Canal through grassy rolling countryside past birch woods and pretty gingerbread houses. Natasha was dressed for the country in an urban pastiche of peasant costume: dainty ankle boots, a white frilly blouse and a flowery patterned skirt, which she hitched up onto her thighs to drive. We had arranged to visit Lavrenty Nikolaevitch, who grew potatoes on his hundred-acre farm. Our plan was to buy him first-generation seed potatoes from the Netherlands. In return, he would give us first option on his crop. He would be protected from a slump in prices, while we would build a business plan on firm foundations.

We got to Dmitrov in the middle of the morning and went to the Tourist Hotel, where we had arranged to meet Lavrenty. Judging from the standard of interior decoration and services such as toilets, it catered for tourists with low expectations of their holiday. Lavrenty was about the same age as me and as unenviably gaunt as I am unenviably plump. All his features – nose, chin, ears, fingers – were long and pointed. Guessing his occupation, you would put him down as undertaker or icon painter and certainly not jolly farmer.

The Union laid on lunch for us in the bleak Soviet dining room. I was now used to having the same meal at any time of day from dawn to midnight: lots of salads and hors d'oeuvres, meat and potatoes, pudding, cake, tea, washed down with vodka, wine, beer and watery fruit juice. So I did justice to the spread at an hour when at home I would be looking forward to a cup of tea and a HobNob. Not my companions, though. I was eating for three. Natasha picked at her food as usual while Lavrenty pushed scraps round his plate.

"The white killer," he said, passing the salt, and I discovered why he looked half starved. He was a food faddist. We got the lecture on salt, sugar, red meat, refined flour, yeast, vinegar, eggs, green vegetables, root vegetables, fruit, you name it. And the man was a farmer. He regarded everything he grew as a threat to humanity. I've met people making cluster bombs for a living who were more in love with their job. When we got up from the table I felt like a bag of toxic waste. On the way out he said something to the manager that only made sense later on: "Please, you may turn the music back on now."

The next chore was a tour of the town before lunch. Mercifully, there was not a lot to see. The historical centre

is the *Kreml* or Kremlin, which means fortress. It was a wall
and moat surrounding two pretty onion-domed cathedrals.
The domes are glossy black and the walls brilliant white,
stylishly monochrome against the clear blue sky. Close by
was a plaque marking the closest the Wehrmacht had got to
Moscow.

We followed Lavrenty out of town and into the countryside. Hedgerows and woods and flower-flecked fields and
ponds with ducks were like a folk memory of the English
countryside before the Common Agricultural Policy
stripped it and raped it yellow. We turned down a corduroy
track made of logs and up to a new and spacious wooden
house with a wide veranda and fretwork round the eaves.

Lavrenty's wife Irene came out to greet us: a buxom,
freckled redhead in a headscarf and apron with apple
cheeks, brawny arms, meaty hands and tree-trunk legs. No
need to guess her occupation, "farmer's wife" sprang
instantly to mind. She was younger than Lavrenty and
clearly impervious to his dietary lectures. In her presence
Lavrenty brightened up as if he tapped into her energy and
cheerfulness. She invited us in, but I asked if we could have
the farm tour first. It looks professional and gets it over
with.

Compared with other farms I had seen this was certainly
well equipped. Lavrenty owned a pick-up, a tractor and
various bits of machinery for digging and scraping and
pushing stuff around and loading things onto other things.
He told us what they were, but as I don't know their names
in English let alone Russian I was none the wiser. There was

a purpose-built shed for potatoes, also empty. This I did know something about. I had been swatting up on the Idaho Potato Board technical leaflets on the subject, so I looked serious and asked intelligent questions about capacity and air circulation and ventilation and damp proofing. He had financed it with Union grants, proof that money was making its way from the state budget to where it was needed.

I asked to inspect the potato fields. We strolled down a grassy track to a pretty meadow surrounded on three sides by forest. With a theatrical sweep of the arm, Lavrenty presented his potato plantation. It was crowded with wild flowers and buzzing with bees and the last butterflies of the season. Natasha took advantage of her outfit to skip through the grass and pick flowers and toss her tousled hair over her shoulder. It was sweet but worrying. I was familiar enough with modern farming to know that wildlife must be exterminated and I asked searching questions about weedkillers and insecticides. Lavrenty was embarrassed and evasive. Union grants and loans did not cover these essentials, which were expensive and in short supply.

With the frown of an expert I popped the key question: Where was the irrigation? Lavrenty took me by the arm and marched me to a concrete culvert beside the road that ran the length of his field.

"The ditch never runs dry. It comes from the river."

"How does the water get from the ditch to the field?"

"By pump."

"Can we see it?"

★

"It is an underwater pump."

"I'd still like to see it."

He gave me the cheerless little smile I have sometimes witnessed and often given in a poker game, when a player folds his cards and with them his stake for the night. Without a word he steered me to a square pit full of water, fed by the stream. Pipes snaked out of it with fitments on the ends for connection to sprayers. I peered into the water.

"Where's the pump, Lavrenty?"

He also peered into the pit, looking puzzled like a man contemplating an empty parking space where all that is left of his car is a few shards of side window glass. He sighed.

"I know. The municipality will not give me the permission. The water goes to Andrei's farm for his fishing."

"Isn't it your water first?"

"Andrei is the Deputy Mayor. What can I do?"

We men walked back to the house subdued. Natasha skipped in the field beside us, oblivious of the dark cloud over our heads. Without weedkiller, fertilizer and irrigation he didn't have a hope of growing a bakeable potato. I burbled on about how lovely the farm was and what a good job he was making of it, but we both knew that his undersized, insect-eaten crop would be good only for street markets.

Another test of diplomacy was waiting for us at the house. Irene clucked and shooed us into the kitchen like chickens at roosting time. On the table was a seventeen-course meal. Most of it originated from the forest and fields and the kitchen garden, which Irene managed with considerably more success than her husband did the rest of the farm. Wild mushrooms and berries and roots, tame vegetables and herbs, rabbit and pigeon from the woods and fowl from the henhouse, home-smoked perch from the river, delicious pies with pastry light as meringue, with creamy horseradish and tangy sour cream, *smetána* – not to be confused, as I often did, with the differently stressed composer Smétana. To drink were the usual watery fruit juice and a fragrant, caraway-flavoured vodka, which their neighbour illegally distilled from Lavrenty's potatoes.

"No salt, no chemicals," said Lavrenty as we sat down, but even this did not induce him to eat anything but boiled potato.

I dug in with a heart as heavy as my stomach. It was only in part because I had finished a slap-up meal just two hours before. This meal was a celebration, prepared for days in advance in honour of our new business relationship. The future of his farm depended on it. When we got to the toast to friendship and cooperation I couldn't look Lavrenty in the eye. The message had not got through to Irene. She piled my plate and talked of what great things Russians and English could do together when they set their mind to it. I complimented her on the farm and her cooking and how farmers like them were pioneers in the resurgence of free Russia, blah blah – remember I was on my second vodka session of the day and it wasn't even tea time.

"But we are not farmers," she said. "I am a nurse. Lavrenty is professor of the accordion."

★

Their story emerged in anecdotes and asides as the day melted into dusk. Lengthening shadows, swirling flocks of roosting birds and the cold orange sun were a suitably elegiac backdrop to the tale.

Lavrenty was the son of two famous accordionists who sometimes played for Stalin. He made his public debut at the age of six before the Father of the People, whom Lavrenty remembered as kind and jolly, beating time on his knee and singing along with the choruses of the patriotic songs. With his parentage and patronage, Lavrenty passed painlessly from Special Musical Primary School through to the Conservatory, where he specialized, like his parents, in the traditional repertoire of the Russian accordion, the *bayan*. This has buttons as opposed to the keys of the Western piano accordion and gives a different sound. He dedicated himself to the works of T. I. Sotnikov, his first tutor and old family friend, who incorporated Russian folk tradition in simple, stirring, optimistic revolutionary themes approved by the Soviet Union of Composers. Sotnikov wrote the very first concerto for *bayan* and symphony orchestra, premiered and alas derniered in 1937. He died in the same year as Stalin, after which his slender reputation withered into a stick from which it has never regrown.

I had the impression that Lavrenty's talent did not flower naturally but was hothoused in other people's expectations. He claimed it was by choice that he took a position in a Musical Secondary School in the provinces and not the prestigious Conservatory. He said that the battle for the *bayan* against the interloping piano accordion, with its tangos and jazz, had to be fought among the young and impressionable. He defended the wholesome repertoire of composers like Sotnikov against the decadence of caco-phonists like Prokofiev and Shostakovich and Schnittke, who had the gall to write a concerto for *bayan*.

Lavrenty settled down, married a colleague, fathered an unmusical daughter. He kept alive the spark of promise his parents had wished on him by entering contests. In 1966 the Soviet Union had ended its self-imposed isolation and stunned the Western world with victories in international accordion contests. Competition to represent the Motherland was intense. In addition to prestige came for-eign travel and currency allowances. The focus of the musi-cal year was the playoffs in Moscow. They were rigged, of course. Contacts, influence, favouritism, a gift or two, a clean sheet with the Union of Composers, ideological soundness – these were what counted for the short list. You also had to be Russian. If you were a Tatar or Cossack or Gypsy forget it, however good you were.

Over the years Lavrenty worked his way up through long lists and short lists to the 1986 final in the Kremlin Theatre. From twelve players six would be chosen to go to Klingenthal in East Germany. Or rather, had already been chosen by the Accordion Committee of the Union of Composers. Lavrenty was one of them.

Over the years, strictures about acceptable music were relaxed. Deviants like Prokofiev and Shostakovich were rehabilitated. Gershwin was allowed. In the 1980s one of the star composers was a woman and a Tatar, Sofia

Gubaidulina. But Lavrenty was too set in his mind and his ways to adapt and he stuck to the old Soviet repertoire. Like countless others in every sphere of life from Leonid Brezhnev down, he stagnated until Gorbachev and *Glasnost* and *Perestroika* swept away the old certainties. There was a revolution in the Accordion Committee and the old guard was ousted. Two months before the concert in the Kremlin Theatre the Berlin Wall fell. The organizers of the Klingenthal delegation were instructed not to include any Soviet works, unless they were by former dissidents.

Lavrenty was in shock. Since the afternoon he had played for Stalin his career had meandered through mediocrity and failure. Klingenthal was his last chance to put things right. His wife had already spent the prize money and the per diem. His daughter had put in an order for a Sony Walkman. He had time to learn new pieces, but when he put a score on the stand the ghosts of his parents stood on either side and jogged his arms to make him play wrong notes. The ghost of T. I. Sotnikov, who had taught him and fought for him and written the music that fed his family, sat in the corner with his hands over his ears.

Lavrenty walked onto the vast stage of the Kremlin Theatre with the calm of despair. In the spotlights he could see no one, only infinite darkness. He donned his accordion, walked up to the microphone and announced that he was not going to play the modern works he was down for in the programme, but an arrangement for single instrument of the *Concerto for Bayan* by T. I. Sotnikov. Out in the bottomless pit he heard a collective intake of breath.

He played like he had never played before. All the promise and expectation of his childhood finally came to fruition. Under his fingers the Russia of his youth in the 1960s melded with the Russia of Sotnikov's youth in the 1920s, full of energy and hope for the world. Lavrenty held the final triumphant chord five times longer than was scored until every last drop of emotion was drained from him. He floated in a dark and silent sea – until a tumultuous wave of applause from the audience lifted him up and brought him triumphantly back to earth. The standing ovation lasted five minutes. The audience was with him: he had played for them all, for their youth, for their Russia. The judges had no choice. They feared for their safety if they denied Lavrenty a ticket to Klingenthal. They also feared for their jobs if he played reactionary Soviet music.

Lavrenty solved their problem. Summoned to the stage to receive first prize by popular acclaim, he was nowhere to be found. He was lost for six months. With the first snows of winter he turned up at the hospital in Dmitrov, half dead from starvation and exposure. He had no memory of where he had been or how he had lived. He was diagnosed as mentally ill and sent to a sanatorium on a collective farm, where the patients worked as part of their therapy. His wife divorced him, his daughter disowned him. He renounced all music, which was why he had asked for the piped music to be turned off in the restaurant that morning.

Irene was a nurse at the sanatorium. It was easy to see why Lavrenty would fall in love with Irene, but not why the affection was reciprocated. It was a classic case of the attraction of opposites. Their chance to make a life together occurred when collective farms were obliged to hand over land to private farmers. Preference went to people already employed by the farms. This was interpreted liberally by the implementing bureaucrats to include themselves, many of whom knew less about farming than I did and used the grants to build nice *dachas* and fence in their land, like Deputy Mayor Andrei. Irene was technically a member of the cooperative that ran the farm and put in an application jointly with Lavrenty. And here they were, finishing each other's sentences, swapping little smiles, being funny about each other, telling themselves how lucky they were.

I excused myself to go to the lavatory and on the way back slipped onto the veranda to watch the sun go down behind the forest. In a film at this point the sound of a distant accordion would waft through the rustlings and chirpings and cawings of dusk. It didn't, thank God. I detest the accordion.

Mixed feelings about the tutu

I should not like to leave you with a false impression of my competence in Russian. My conversations were not as crisp and coherent as they have been reported. I was diligent with *Teach Yourself Russian* and practised on strangers in the street, but even when I got the words right first time I mixed up the vowels and put the stresses in the wrong place. People I talked to had a permanent air of puzzlement. For someone in my business the similarity between *kartoshka* (potato) and *kartochka* (business card) was a frequent source of confusion at first meetings. I looked for a language teacher and answered an advertisement in the *Moscow Times*. Anna: Russian Conversation and/or Ballet Lessons.

I have mixed feelings about the tutu. When I was 15 the church youth club had a fancy dress party. I persuaded my balletomanic sister to lend me her outfit. Although I am three years older and my nickname at school was Fatty, my sister, now svelte and elegant, was also on the tubby side. Whenever I see Walt Disney's ballet-dancing hippopotamuses I am transported to languid summer afternoons and her performances on the

★

lawn. So the tutu fitted, sort of. I can still feel the *frisson* of an itchy one-piece satin body stocking and its nylon frills, the pink tights, the bodice, the Dunlop tennis pumps, the powder and lipstick, the wand with a silver star. At a different school from the rest of the club and a loner, I didn't know that all the others had chickened out of fancy dress. I made a triumphant and excruciating entrance. The club was only ten minutes from my house and I could have run home and changed into Norwegian sweater and twill trousers, but I am proud that I stuck it out for the whole evening, sod them.

The Pope died that night. Radio Luxembourg interrupted the Top 20 countdown to announce that he was *in extremis*. Father Raymund broke up the jiving and we all gathered round in a circle to pray, a Franciscan in a habit, fifty youths and the Sugar Plum Fairy. From that night on the recurrent nightmare of walking round in public wearing nothing but a vest too short to pull down was replaced forever by appearing on stage in a knickerless tutu whose rigid disk rises at the back when you push it down at the front and vice versa. So the ballet has a special resonance for me. I come to it with heightened sensitivity, all the shame and anger and sexual ambivalence of that night heaped on the performance.

Anna had been a dancer with the Bolshoi and now worked in an office. She was in her early 40s and although plump and round, still had the poise and scraped-back hair of a ballerina. She also had lovely brown eyes and a jolly smile. I went to her on Wednesday evenings for conversation without dancing.

We hit it off at our first meeting. She ushered me into her living room and on the sideboard next to the samovar was a black-and-white photograph of a *corps de ballet* doing its thing. I peered at it.

"Oh, it's *Giselle*," I said, "and that's you leading the Wilis. Don't you look marvellous?"

Did she blossom? I could have swept her into a Lukom lift if the ceiling had been high enough.

Despite my negative attitude to ballet in general, I am an expert on *Giselle*. I had been only three times to live ballet, all in the space of a week. When I first arrived in Moscow Misha got tickets for *Giselle* at the Bolshoi. In St Petersburg we were treated to *Giselle* at the Mariinsky, to crackly recorded music. Back in Moscow we were invited to a Sunday-night gala performance of *Giselle* at the Kremlin Theatre. I couldn't get the damn tunes out of my head for weeks. The plot is based on the idea that girls who die on their wedding day become wicked fairies called Wilis. There is an unforgettable bit in the second act when the Wilis stand in Indian file on one leg, bend into an arabesque and do a sort of hop and shuffle forward, like the Egyptian sand dance that Flanagan and Allan did in the music hall. I used to look forward to it as a bit of light relief, but everyone else took it seriously and applauded and I learned not to giggle. And lo, on the sideboard was Anna leading the charge of the Wilis, a seraphic smile on her face.

From then on I was her favourite pupil. I hid my ignorance of the rest of the repertoire behind my impoverished Russian and although she gave me strange looks from time

★

to time, for example when I mixed up *La Sylphide* and *Les Sylphides* or Swanilda and the Black Swan, she gave me the benefit of the doubt.

Anna's husband Pavel worked at the Patent Office. He was younger than her. On the evidence of a colour photograph on the other side of the samovar from the sand-dancing Wilis, he was a martial arts expert. He struck a fearsome pose, a bald man in white pyjamas about to break an invisible brick in half. Was it my imagination or did I see evidence of practice on the fixtures and fittings, a cracked Formica table top, a splintered cupboard door, dents in the walls? He was her second husband. The first had something to do with set design, but whether on the artistic or the artisanal side my vocabulary was not good enough to tell.

Yuri, their 18-year old son, lived with his father in a flat in the Bolshoi complex behind the theatre, a self-contained village for a thousand people.

"Does Yuri dance?"

"Like an elephant. He builds computers. He is a good boy. He prefers to be with me but he gets a better schooling over there. He comes to see me if he doesn't have too much homework. He works very hard."

She sounded so brave and her brown eyes were so sad that I wanted to put my arm round her and give her a hug, but she might have misinterpreted the gesture.

One evening after our lesson she invited me to stay for supper and meet Pavel. She would not let me help her lay the low table in the overstuffed living room, saying I should try to behave like a Russian. There were pilchards and ten different vegetables, including potatoes fried in goose fat and some succulent home-preserved mushrooms, diluted fruit juice of course and half a bottle of Stolichnaya from the back of the sideboard cupboard. Anna fussed and fluttered and was full of apologies that she had no caviar or sturgeon or meat or wine to offer me, but Pavel said they couldn't afford it. I was rescued from embarrassment by the clanking of the lift and the clunking of the steel door that announced his arrival. We sat straight down to eat.

Pavel was careworn but put on a brave face. He was not totally bald, although his very fair hair and pale skin made him seem so. He had deep-set black eyes, which I imagined could be intimidating on the other side of a fighting mat. He took the offensive with an explanation of the differences between Russian and British patent law and then between the various types of martial art. I fought back with potato varieties of the world.

In a lull, while we picked our teeth, Anna brightly announced to Pavel that she had managed to get two tickets for the Bolshoi the following Thursday night. Back of the stalls, no less.

"Excellent," he mumbled, still working on a back molar, "I can get forty dollars for them outside."

"No, Pavel, it's the Gala. If they see you I will never get tickets again. And I want to go. You know I always go."

"I can't go," he said, "there's a tournament up at Dynamo."

"You never come these days."

94

"I can't. I just said. That's enough." He pointed a morsel of impaled pilchard at me. "Take Ivan. It will get his mind off Maris Pipers."

Anna raised her immaculately plucked eyebrows at me. "Will you come?"

"Is it *Giselle*?"

"Oh, I'm sorry. I know it's your favourite. No, it's the Gala. It is a concert given by the final year of the ballet school. They are so wonderful."

I'd have preferred to go with Pavel to Dynamo, but her pleading brown eyes were irresistible.

I picked Anna up at her apartment on the Thursday. She seemed pleased that I was sporting a dark suit and tie. She wore a black skirt, a low-cut blouse and a short jacket made of fluffy white feathers. It was only her dancer's poise and grooming that saved her from looking like a Muppet. To avoid squashing the jacket under her overcoat she put it into a plastic bag with her high heels. She was made up for the stage in yellow-orange foundation and bright red lipstick and I sensed this was a special occasion, so I was glad I had kept the taxi.

It was a nice change to have an audience of Russians in the Bolshoi instead of boorish foreign tourists like me. Even I couldn't match the remark I heard at my first *Giselle* from an American to his wife: "Gee, the hang time on the jumps was piss-poor stacked up against them Mongols at the circus." A third of the audience were related to the performers and a third were former pupils and dancers like Anna. The rest were connected in some way to the company or the industry, so it was a festive atmosphere that infected even me. Best of all were the dancers. Their training had not yet squeezed out their enthusiasm, their pleasure in dancing, their sheer exuberance. They did the old favourites, but you had the feeling that this was a First Night, that anything could happen, unlike professional performances that are as spontaneous as Trooping the Colour.

Anna was on her feet with the rest at the end of every act, clapping until her hands were red raw, smiling her crinkly smile, her lovely brown eyes moist with emotion. Of course she was cheering on the new generation, but I suspected she was also applauding herself as she was then, the stage and life immense before her. I imagined her up there dancing for the woman she would become in her chicken-feather outfit and bright red lipstick. Once again I wanted to give her a hug, but she might have misinterpreted the gesture.

At the interval we bustled off to the main bar where she met old dancing partners. With advancing years dancers either turn into death's heads with sunken eyes and flesh-less bones or into fairies who have overdone the sugar plums. They gathered under the giant chandelier, elegant little women with scraped-back hair, feet in the turned-out position, arms in the first or, for those with handbags, in the third, and one or two *sur le cou-de-pied*, for all the world as if they were rhubarbing in a crowd scene twenty-five years before. I bought them champagne and canapés, which they sipped and nibbled like little birds.

★

After innumerable curtain calls and tears and bravos and showers of flowers, kisses and lingering farewells while the ushers and cleaners tried to empty the place, Anna took my arm in the queue for coats. It was still early. I would have liked to take her out to dinner, but it would have been obscene to spend the equivalent of Pavel's monthly salary or more and might have been misinterpreted. Instead, I stopped the taxi at a roadside kiosk on the way to her apartment and bought a couple of bottles of champagne and delicacies like Frito-Lay chips and corned beef.

Pavel was not yet home. Anna put her chicken suit back on, I opened the champagne and we toasted the Bolshoi, the Big One.

"Tell me what it was like when you joined. How did it feel?"

"I was six years old. That morning is like yesterday, it was snowing, and my mother said it was the last time I would wear felt boots, from now on they would give me leather for my feet. It was not true, of course. I was scared, but no more than going to a birthday party. And it was a party for twenty years, although we worked very hard."

She took a scrapbook down from the top shelf and sat next to me on the narrow sofa. The chicken feathers smelled of camphor and tickled my nose, but it was not unpleasant to have her pressed up next to me, balancing the book on our knees and clinking our glasses every now and then, flicking through programmes and cuttings and photographs. She pointed out children who had defected to the West or died, and some I had just met at the theatre.

"Why did you leave?"

"I was divorced. I could have stayed and worked in the administration, but I didn't want to. My husband was an attractive man. There are many pretty young girls in the Bolshoi. One of the little rats got her teeth into him. I know it's normal, but I didn't want to stay."

"Where did you meet Pavel?"

"In the metro. He had nothing to do with ballet. It was my defection."

"Martial arts is a kind of ballet, isn't it?"

"Don't let Pavel hear you say that. For him it is war. He only took it up when things got worse. He used to be a gentle person when he had a good job. Now he is angry."

"How did he lose his job?"

"He didn't. It's the same job. Good jobs became bad jobs. He thinks that when he is a martial arts master he will get a job as a bodyguard. But what good are hands and sticks against guns? He should buy an Uzi and go and practise in the forest."

"How does he get on with Yuri?"

"He never sees him. I would have liked a child with Pavel, but who can afford children these days?"

This was getting too melancholy. "Show me how you dance. Show me the positions."

"Oh John, I can't. I am not a dancer any more."

"In here you are a *prima ballerina assoluta*. Come on."

We pushed the low table back and she kicked off her high heels. She ran through the five classical positions and their variations, then the *écarté*, the *éffacé*, the *croisé* and more. She was still very supple and altogether transformed. It was getting very hot and I removed my jacket and tie. Anna took off her feather jacket.

"Can you hold your foot and lift your leg up straight?"

"You mean the *détiré?* Oh John, not in these clothes. In English you call this shouldering the leg." Her eyes blazed for a moment and then she giggled.

"What clothes do you need?"

"The tutu."

"Do you still have your old tutus?"

"Of course."

"Let me see them. Please."

Leading straight off the dining room was a small room, big enough for a narrow single bed, a fitted cupboard and a desk. The bed was kept made up for Yuri. On the wall hung a Tae Kwon Do stick. I followed her inside. She burrowed in the cupboard and came out with parcels wrapped in tissue paper. We sat side by side on the bed and she carefully unwrapped each one.

"This is the Romantic tutu, like we wear in your favourite *Giselle.* See, it flows down to the calf. And this is the Classical tutu I wore in *Swan Lake.* The frill is separate now but you sew it onto the bodice."

"Will you put it on?"

"Oh, I was a young girl then. Here, I'll put on the headdress."

She picked up the confection of tulle and ribbon, the white now faded to yellow, and put it on. Suddenly her eyes welled with tears and she sobbed, her hands folded on her breast, head turned aside, in the classical mime for love. We heard the clanking of the lift and the clunking of the steel door and she went back into the living room to open the door.

"Oh my flower, what has happened to your face?"

"I lost my bout. Who is here? What is all this? Have you had an orgy?" His voice was very loud and getting louder.

"It's only John."

I thought for a second it was a set-up. The misunderstood wife yearning for love, the violent husband, a honey trap like in the good old days of the Cold War. They had preyed on my innocence and now they would prey on my wallet. And what was worse, who could blame them, impoverished by the likes of me and our phony economics, our money seducing away their talent, filling their theatres with boors and their offices with charlatans?

"My honey bear, sit down."

"Where is your poxy Westerner, then?" The word he used for Westerner was *spidonosets*, AIDS carrier.

I made my entrance. Pavel was tussling with Anna, who was trying to bathe his face with champagne. There was a purple bruise down one side and the eye was half closed. I stood in the doorway in the fifth position, legs crossed, feet turned out as much as they would go, *les bras en haut*, the classical tutu tucked into my waistband, the ribbons of the headdress dangling over my face.

"Darlings, how do I look?"

They stared at me amazed, half in wonderment, half in fear. I had never seen Anna's brown eyes nor Pavel's good one so wide.

★

"Hah," he shouted, "I told you! Didn't I tell you? These English are gay! Everybody knows."

"Actually it's for the British Embassy Club fancy dress. Honestly."

"When a man says honestly he is not honest. But we are broad-minded. No wonder Anna likes you, she spent too long with ballet dancers. But for God's sake take that stuff off before I throw up. Keep it for your English lover-boys."

It was a victory of sorts. Anna went unhappily to bed and Pavel put Bruce Lee on the video. We drank champagne with vodka chasers until I staggered out into the night in search of a taxi. I wrote to Anna the next day thanking her for a wonderful evening and enclosing forty dollars for Pavel.

We swim in tide of history

I t was fine to trudge around the streets of Moscow incognito in skiing anorak and pixie hat, but I felt the outfit was beneath the dignity of an international development consultant and restaurateur. It was time for a wardrobe renewal. The obvious solution was an overcoat and a *shapka*, a fur hat.

I went shopping in GUM. It is pronounced Goom and stands for *Gosudarstvenny Universalny Magazin*, State Universal Store. Forming one side of Red Square opposite Lenin's tomb, GUM was the first shopping mall of modern times, a magnificent nineteenth-century iron-and-glass conservatory on two floors with arcades and balconies and a fountain. When I first went there it was a wonderful bazaar, full of exotic pilgrims from all over the Soviet Union. Duty done by the corpse of Comrade Lenin, after hours of queuing often in the bitter cold, it was their reward to hurry across the square and join the scrum for household goods and fabrics and the latest Russian fashions. They agonized over two types of boots or two styles of dress, the white plates or the yellow plates, the red flowers or the blue. Far from being patronizing over the limited selection, I envied them the simplicity of choice.

There were still some of the old stores left, on hard times now that the pilgrims no longer came and street traders undercut them. But the rest were being privatized and GUM had set up a real-estate office. A German supermarket sold clothes and Dior had a shop.

My first purchase was easy. For a ridiculously low price I bought a dark-blue overcoat in thick wool, with a fake-fur detachable lining. It was the kind of coat that stood for hours on top of the Lenin mausoleum without feeling the chill as the rockets went by. When I took it off it was like the trick where several people press down on your head and shoulders – they take their hands away and you rise to the ceiling at the touch of a finger.

The *shapka* was another matter. There was certainly a choice, from dyed rabbit to mink. But I have to report that despite appearances to the contrary, Russians do not have big heads. While fur hats create an illusion of the hydrocephalic Slav, the bonce underneath is around size seven. This was a grievous disappointment to a size seven-and-three-quarters who had to have my school caps made to measure. When I was drafted into the school cadet force not even the British Army had a big enough beret. Throughout life I have had to go without baseball caps and panamas and cycling helmets and sombreros, and now I was to be denied a *shapka*.

All day I traipsed round GUM, the street markets, the tourist shops, without success. As Russian milliners hadn't caught on to the idea of putting sizes in hats, they made me try on all their stock. Assistants tugged at the rims, incredulous managers brought tape measures, stock boys ransacked their storerooms, but every specimen of animal skin perched on my head like a cat on a cushion. I was depressed. Was this was a portent of my Russian adventure? If the cap fits wear it. And if it doesn't fit?

My way home passed the Moscow Cinema Centre. The main screen was showing the new Bruce Willis and was sold out. I loitered with the crowd on the steps and sidled up to people asking if they had a spare ticket to sell. In my new coat I must have looked like a tout, because several hopefuls asked how much I was selling for. The lucky ticket holders drifted inside and I was left alone.

"My friend, you want movie? Come," said a man behind me in English. He was slight, wiry, about 35, Mexican moustache, dark eyes, shabby grey suit, no coat or hat, nice small head. He led the way round the side of the cinema. Thinking he was slipping me through an emergency exit for a couple of bucks, I followed, but he opened the door into an office building. Not wishing to be found the next day minus wallet, new coat and several pints of blood, I turned back.

"Come, please. Classic movie."

"I don't watch porno."

"Not porno. Great movie."

"I don't watch snuff." Especially my own.

"*Hey You Goose*. Lydia Bobrova. Very good Russian movie. Astakhov kinematographer. Nominated for Golden

Leopard in Locarno." For a mugger he knew his movies. It meant nothing: muggers go to the pictures too. "Ten dollars."

"Ten dollars! I don't pay that in London."

"Five dollars, then. And if you like movie you take home for fifty dollars."

This I couldn't resist. We took the lift to the fifth floor, which had been opulent in its day, with white beech panelling, red carpet and frosted-glass wall lights. It seemed we were the only ones on the floor, if not the building. I followed him down a corridor to a pair of double doors. He opened one with a flourish and ushered me into a small viewing room with a dozen rows of what the Streatham Odeon calls *fauteuils* and pronounces footles.

"Five dollars. Thank you. Sit down where you like. When reel wants change I am 502."

The lights dimmed, the screen flickered and I was treated to a personal viewing of *Hey You Goose*, with English subtitles, in black and white, moving and funny, set in a provincial village at the time of the 1980 Olympics. The hopeless lives of the villagers contrasted with the hype and hoopla of the Olympics. When the projector clattered into white mist I went to fetch my projectionist down the corridor in room 502. On the second reel he was sitting at a desk opposite a plump, dyed blonde with jet-black eyebrows, a serious squint and an overbite. On the third reel they were on the same side of the desk dealing with a bottle of vodka and he had his jacket off. When the film finished I coughed and knocked loudly. They were flushed, but it could have

★

been the vodka. Leonid searched for a glass in the bottom drawer of the desk while the woman kindly took my coat and bags and pulled up a chair for me.

"I am Leonid. This Marta. I am PhD in English Linguistics. We are scream-writers. You?"

"*Biznismyen*."

"We are *biznismyen* too. We have made the Intercinema Agency – Insultant Services for Film Production, Distributing and Advertisements in Russia. What is your business?"

"Fast-food restaurants."

"We have two tons of frozen meat. Pork, beef, chicken," said Marta. Because of her squint she addressed an empty space about 45 degrees off, aggravating my growing sense of displacement.

"What?"

"We make publicity movie for the Saratov Machine Tool Company. They pay us frozen meat. Only three years old. Very fine."

I didn't want to talk about catering. I asked if they made much of a living by ambushing film buffs in the street. Wasn't there a more conventional way of attracting customers?

"I only had idea when I saw you. Our first idea is to sell films. You want to buy the film? Fifty dollars."

"Don't the films belong to the Film Centre?"

"Nobody watches them no more. They want porno. Bruce Villis. Gollivud."

"I'd love to, but I don't have a projector. Why don't you advertise and get people to see them? You could get fifty dollars and keep the film."

We planned a marketing programme built around small ads in the English-language papers. I undertook to finance the first four insertions in return for free admission for life. To seal our new partnership, Marta went away and returned with sausage and a loaf of bread. I felt good about my part in saving the *cinémathèque* for posterity.

We toasted friendship and success and world cinema. We concocted the plot for a comedy, to be co-produced in Britain and Russia, about an Englishman, a no-hoper and dreamer with a distorted and romantic idea of Russia, who comes to Moscow to try his luck and escape his creditors and pretends to be a wealthy *biznismyen.* He falls in with a Russian no-hoper and dreamer with a romantic and dis-torted idea of the West, who pretends to be well connected with the new *nomenklatura.* They con each other and try to set up a fast-food restaurant. They fancy the same woman and each thinks the other is sleeping with her. The mafia steps in and the business collapses. The girl brings them together, they save each other from the mafia and they plan another venture.

"Darling," said Leonid, "we have first draft scream-play in three days. I know everybody in film business. We start shooting in six months. Please, you find pre-financing."

"No problem. I'll put it to my investors. I'm sure the British Board of Film Finance will come in as well," I said, stepping into the character of our hero.

"How about fifty dollars for immediate expenses?" asked Marta of an empty space two yards to my left. I pretended she wasn't talking to me.

Leonid talked about the smuggled foreign films they had watched as aspirant screenwriters. Comedy was his speciality and he knew the early Carry On films almost off by heart. *Carry On Camping* was his favourite. Unlike Leonid, Marta had actually worked in films before the industry died through lack of state financing. She talked about the actors she had worked with and sighed and implied that she had slept with them, but I fear it was brave talk. We bemoaned the invasion of Gollivud and the collapse of Russian cinema. I talked about A. A. Tarkovsky's *Andrei Rublev* and *Solaris* and *Stalker* and *The Sacrifice* – I didn't confess I found them hard going.

We got to the last half inch or so in the bottle, the moment for sentimentality before you toss the empty into the bin and life goes on. I told them the story of my day. I tried to make it funny, but I felt my eyes burn and a vodka-laced tear trickle down my cheek as I recalled my big head and the humiliation it had caused, from the day my mother sent me to the infant school round the corner in one of her pink sunhats, to standing hatless on the parade ground with 400 boys in berets, to having a crone in GUM prod the bumps on my head and tut.

I sniffled and wiped my eyes. It was all so not as it should be. Leonid and Marta looked at me – at least I assume Marta did – and their eyes filled too, astonished at a display of emotion from an Englishman. They talked quickly to each other in low voices, too quickly for me to understand, and I didn't care. Marta left the room. Leonid filled our glasses and tossed the bottle in the bin. We slugged the vodka down without a word. Leonid sighed. Marta came back. In her arms she cradled what looked like an obese cat. Looking over my shoulder she held it out to me. It was a hat, not fur but Astrakhan, thick tight curls of black wool. In all other respects it was a proper *shapka* with earflaps tied over the top with black tapes.

"Try it."

"I can't."

"Trust me."

It wasn't new, but there were no unpleasant sweat marks on the band inside or hair-oil stains on the lining. It was heavy. With two hands, like Napoleon crowning himself, I put it on. It was a perfect fit. I had never worn such a hat. A hat that doesn't sit on your head but envelops it. A hat that you do not wear, it wears you. Heavy and solid. There was no forgetting you had it on. I stood bolt upright because it threw me off balance if I stooped.

Leonid applauded, his face creased with genuine pleasure. Marta looked smugly into space. She pointed to a mirror on the back of the door. I looked like the minotaur with a man's body and a gigantic woolly head.

"Where did it come from?"

"Andrei Konchalovsky. When he go to Gollivud for *Tango and Cash* he give it to archive. Big head."

"Can I have it?"

"Of course," said Marta, "Fifty dollars."

A bargain. The cap fitted. And next Saturday the *ciné-mathèque* was full of foreigners paying five bucks to see subtitled Russian classics, as advertised in the *Moscow Times*.

★

took my hat for a walk. It was the end of autumn. An occasional flurry of snow dusted the slush underfoot and the temperature touched freezing in the middle of the night, but during the day it was mild and sunny. The political climate was more sinister, however. Revolution was in the air. An emergency session of the Congress of People's Deputies had been called to impeach President Yeltsin. The Communists were poised to take back power and renounce what they called "political adventurism and romanticism about democracy". The German Chancellor warned of the threat to Germany if Yeltsin was toppled. The G7 called an emergency session. The European papers ran profiles of army generals and whether they were likely to stay in their barracks.

When I went out that sunny Sunday morning I didn't anticipate spending the day at the epicentre of world-shaking events. I felt like a stroll round the icons at the new Tretyakov Gallery, a chocolate sundae in Red Square, a sub-titled film at the Moscow Film Centre and a couple of pints of Guinness and a steak-and-kidney pie at Rosie O'Grady's. It was a lovely day. Sunday bells were ringing and the sun shone from a china-blue sky on frosted walls and golden cupolas. My Astrakhan hat was a bit hot and itchy, but I had exchanged the commissar's coat for an anorak. Looking like a native was not only vanity but protection from harassment. The currency touts and taxi drivers outside the museum ignored me.

The Tretyakov is about half an hour's pleasant walk from Red Square on the other side of the Moskva River. I sauntered back musing on icons, wishing I could learn to like them more, as to me one Dormition looks pretty much like another. I crossed the wide bridge to the sloping square in front of the Rossiya Hotel and behind St Basil's to see a crowd scene from a jigsaw puzzle, masses of white dots for faces and swirling red-white-and-blue flags against the candy-coloured domes of the cathedral. What their PA system lacked in clarity it made up for in volume. Ranting speeches were punctuated by cheers and applause and blasts of patriotic music. Megaphones and car horns and a jazz band added to the gaiety.

Up closer the scene was less coherent and lively than it appeared from the other side of the river. People milled around and chatted and ate ice cream and ignored the speeches. The cheering and applause came canned from the loudspeakers. From time to time a rabble rouser took the mike and tried to get a chant going, "Yeltsin Yeltsin Yeltsin", but only a few enthusiasts in front of the podium joined in. Claques of students made the most noise. We were a varied lot, of all ages and types, as many older people in shabby clothes as youngsters in expensive jackets and jeans. Couples flirted and took photos of each other. Men wore dark jackets and medal ribbons. Vendors mooched around trying to sell badges and souvenirs and postcards, but business was poor except for paper flags. I bought a lapel badge from a gypsy-looking fellow who grumbled about the tourists being scared away.

The only seriously motivated people were those who formed two queues snaking through the crowd, each over

★

100 yards long, for the His and Hers lavatory trucks parked by the end of the bridge. The toilets were simple constructions, a shed divided into five compartments on top of a trailer with a metal container underneath. Each cubicle had an open window from which refinements such as frosted glass or curtains had long since disappeared. The Hers truck was placed so that the windows faced the bridge in full view of pedestrians. You saw the back of a woolly hat just above the sill and then the owner stood up and a white bum filled the frame. Knickers were hoisted – I can report various shades of pink and beige – followed by a flurry of movement and another woolly hat appeared. An occasional passer-by would loiter on the bridge for a better look, but the unselfconscious mooning was generally ignored.

I was curious to see what was happening at the other end of Red Square. It was barricaded off and all the streets around were blockaded with trucks and buses full of young militiamen smoking and sleeping sweetly on each other's shoulders. In contrast, GUM was open and full of shoppers indifferent to history. On the way through I stocked up on a cheese pie and a Pepsi in case the government fell and they sealed off Rosie O'Grady's.

The anti-Yeltsin faction was assembled in Manezh Square between the Moscow Hotel and the old Lenin Museum. Although the museum was closed for renovation and Leninism banished to the Revolution Museum on Tverskaya, it was still the regular meeting place for die-hard Communists. They had assembled about half as many people as the democrats. It was the same mix of young and old, shabby and smart, with a greater proportion of old men wearing dark jackets and medal ribbons. They looked more careworn and unhealthy than the others, possibly because they were not enjoying the sweets of the enterprise economy. Their allegiances were more fragmented than the democrats'. There were hammer-and-sickle flags, black-white-and-yellow flags, black-white-and-yellow flags with Imperial eagles, white flags with Imperial eagles. I was so used to seeing the red flag as a tourist souvenir that it was a shock to see it waved in earnest. There were a lot more homemade placards and banners than on the other side and newspapers that looked as if they had been printed on the same presses as Lenin's *Iskra*, "The Spark". The Communists quaintly called each other *tavarish*, comrade.

Different factions of the anti-democrats had different PA systems. Wails of feedback were interspersed with lonely chants of "Yeltsin Out" and "Long Live Lenin" and "Bring Back the Romanovs", but they got nowhere with the crowd who milled around and ate ice cream and ignored the poor badge vendors and postcard sellers. Again, the only ones with any sense of purpose shuffled forwards in the His and Hers queues that snaked among the crowd. The anti-Yeltsin lavatories were parked in the shade around the corner from the Tomb of the Unknown Soldier. From the steps of the museum I was able to ascertain that the bottoms were as large and the knickers the same colours as those of the democrats.

I was thinking of leaving history to play out without me when I recognized a neighbour at the front of the Hers

★

queue, a sweet old *babushka* who lived in the effluvium of drains and cat and cabbage in the bilges of my staircase. I sometimes helped her down with her shopping and breathing through the mouth did no good at all. She was little and dumpy and had ice-blue eyes and beautiful white hair tucked neatly into a purple woolly hat. Strung round her neck she carried a picture of Comrade Stalin that must have hung on her wall. Most days she loitered in our square looking as if she was trying to remember where she lived and I would not have associated her with political activism. We greeted each other like long-lost relatives.

"Comrade Olga, how are things?"

"Normal. The queue moves so slowly that as soon as I have my widdle I have to go to the back and start again. Why are you here? Why aren't you with the Americans on the other side?"

"When I was at university the Communists had the best parties."

"The girls were hotter, eh? Just like us." For a sweet old lady she had a dirty laugh.

"Was he your boyfriend?" I asked, tapping the picture on her chest.

"My husband crawled on his belly from the Volga to the Elbe for this man. He kept the country together. Look what's happening to us now."

"But Comrade Stalin did terrible things to Russians."

"You don't understand."

"You're right." I could never understand. What people like her had been through was outside every frame of reference available in the leafy postwar suburbs of Birmingham.

We reached the steps up to the trailer and I said goodbye. I didn't think it was polite to hang around while a friend mooned out of the window. I hankered after another cheese pie and strolled back into GUM. Through the ground-floor windows it looked as if the democrats were becoming livelier, so I went out at the St Basil's end. People were pushing closer towards the Kremlin walls and there was talk that Yeltsin was going to make an appearance. I was at the edge of a group chanting "Yeltsin Yeltsin" in a desultory sort of way when I saw a pretty blonde girl in a skiing jacket pushing through the throng in apparent distress.

"Please, does anybody here speak English?"

"Yes, me," I said.

"Oh, thank God," she gasped.

I gripped her upper arms with a brotherly sort of embrace, which she tried hard to wriggle out of.

"Calm down. Don't worry. Tell me what's happened. We'll find help. Take deep breaths. It's all right."

"Let go! We are the BBC. Please, will you come with me?"

Still thinking there had been a terrible accident, I followed her through the crowd. We pushed through a cordon of police towards an angular frame and crinkly smile familiar from countless *Newsnight*s. Anticipating the worst of the physical as well as the political climate, he wore an extravagant pair of calf-length thick brown fur moon boots. He had his back to the Mr Whippy domes of St Basil's, protected by gun-toting *milizia* savvy enough to stay out of shot. He waved cheerily and beckoned me over to a little group of young people next to him.

"Ah, super. Very good. Are we ready?"

It was only when he looked into a camera that I realized what was going on. His expression suddenly became earnest, his eyes bulged, he put heavy stress on alternate syllables whether it made sense or not, and he jerked his head this way and that while keeping his eyes fixed on the camera, as they are taught in TV Presenters' School, so they don't look wooden but afflicted with nervous tics.

"A CRUcial VOTE for BORis YELtsin. ALL day THERE have BEEN DEMonSTRATions HERE in RED Square…"

What was I going to do? The sweet blonde girl in the ski jacket smiled nervously at us. Oh why not, what the hell. Besides, I felt uniquely qualified as a *vox populi* since I had been even-handedly demonstrating on both sides. It all went very quickly and in a blur. The younger Russians spoke like Americans. And then he turned to me, asked me why I was demonstrating today and stuck the microphone under my nose as if he were offering me a lick of his cornet. Taking inspiration from my hat, I palatalized my laterals and vocalized my fricatives and tried to sound like a local.

"*Znachet*, we cannot go back. We swim in tide of history."

I thought I had been rumbled. A man with an earpiece waved his hands. The sweet blonde girl was cutting her own throat with what I hoped was only her finger. Our correspondent whipped the microphone away and stared earnestly at the lens.

★

"FROM MosCOW in TURmoil NOW back TO the STUDio."

I was told that the Beeb used my interview for the next two days. A couple of newspapers borrowed the cliché about the tide of history and used it as a photo caption. Otherwise I would have found it hard to believe that I had been in the same place as the journalists who described that day. They said that 60,000 Yeltsin supporters took to the streets and 10,000 Communists and Nationalists. That many would have filled Old Trafford, but I never saw any more than you'd have got at St Andrews for a midweek Birmingham City game. And the democrats certainly did not outnumber the Communists by six to one. It was two to one more like and possibly closer.

That was not the first or the last time that I found it hard to match media stories with what actually goes on in Russia. The only incontrovertible fact I can report is that the knickers on both sides were the same shades of pink and beige.

Spuds and bugs

I met my first Russian in 1984. George Orwell's shadow hung over us. Chernenko was the moribund President of the moribund Soviet Union. Famous Russian dissidents were in exile, Sakharov in the closed city of Gorky, Solzhenitsyn in Vermont. The Soviet Union boycotted the Los Angeles Olympics as the Americans had done to Moscow in 1980. Ronald Reagan was cranking up the Cold War with the Hollywoodesque Strategic Defense Initiative "Star Wars". He armed what would now be called terrorists against Soviet-backed Third World governments: Unita in Angola, the Contras in Nicaragua, the Taliban in Afghanistan. James Bond was still pitted against the Russians. Russia was another world, alien, strange and threatening.

Vladimir was a young biochemist on a six-month exchange programme. A mutual acquaintance introduced us. My wife and I were about to go on a package tour to Leningrad and Moscow and jumped at the chance to practise dealing with the enemy. We invited him round to the house for dinner. This was big news in the playground, the office and the pub. Russians were exotic. The children were excited and we were nervous.

We hit it off. Vladimir looked more English than I did in sports jacket and flannels, except that his Pringle pullover was too clean and his flannels too pressed and his brogues too polished. He was a few years younger than us with a three-year-old daughter and a baby he had never seen, born while he was in the UK. He spoke fluent English and was delightful company, with a sense of humour tinged with pessimism and irony. He was disarmingly frank about the conditions at home, good and bad. The KGB had warned him that foreign agents would try to recruit him. He should be careful of gifts and invitations to dinner from strangers. We grew up suspicious of Russians, especially semi-diplomats like trade delegates and exchange scientists, but we refused to be browbeaten by fears dinned into us by our governments.

The test came when we offered to take presents to Moscow for his new baby. We hadn't bargained for letters and cassettes. Were we couriers of scientific secrets? Were we being set up? At the same time, Vladimir had similar misgivings. Was this a trap? All of us made the same conscious decision: sod it, we were not going to be bullied by propaganda.

I confess I was nervous when the stony-faced customs officer took the letters and tapes into a back room for twenty minutes. When he came back he had a grin on his face. Still, Vladimir did not risk foreigners going to his flat. His neighbours were scandalized by his going abroad and he had relatives in the army who disapproved. He asked colleagues from his laboratory to pick up the things. Our anxieties might have been laughable, but there was no mistaking the fear of the two young men who came to the lobby of the Intourist Hotel. They snatched the bags from us and ran out without a word. We felt sorry for them and sorry for all of us. It all sounds risible now, but in those days it seemed serious.

After we came back from Russia we had strange phone calls and clicks on the line. They were probably more to do with the incompetence of British Telecom than surveillance, but we thought they might have been more sinister. Mail we received from Vladimir was definitely opened, but who had done the tampering we had no idea. Over the years we exchanged Christmas cards and I sent him my books. In Moscow I got in touch and he invited me for dinner. I was to meet him at his Institute.

The Institute was a ten-minute walk from Gagarin Square. The first man in space stood on top of a flare-shaped silver column, reaching for the stars. Since his day Russian science had fallen on hard times. The Institute was run down, weeds growing in the cracks, peeling paint, post-Patriotic-War functional and not changed much since. The lobby led to a cascade of marble steps going up to a landing. A lady of the same vintage as the guard swabbed them with a rag tied on a stick, refreshing it every now and then in a bucket of filthy water. Halfway through she stopped for a rest, leaning on the mop and looking at her threadbare slippers. Water plink-plonked down the steps. A grandiose clock over the door had stopped at ten past nine.

Time had been better to Vladimir. He looked exactly as he had when we'd last met in London a decade before. We asked how the other was: *Not so bad* and *Normalna* were the verdicts. He took me on a tour. The landing was decorated with mug shots of professors dating back to the foundation of the Institute in 1935. Even the more recent looked like people from another time, stern faced, some in military uniform.

"You know Oparin, of course," said Vladimir. "Darwin of the twentieth century."

He showed me the great man's laboratory. Like all the other labs it was a disappointment. It had a couple of wooden tables, a few test tubes and other bits and pieces out of a decent chemistry set.

"He developed the primal soup theory of the origin of life. He was a big friend of Salvador Dali."

I tried to infuse the shabby little room with the surreal mysteries of the universe. All I could think was that it could have done with a bit of a dust.

"It has not changed since he died in 1980. We do not have the money to change anything. When the Soviet Union collapsed our funding collapsed."

"Bang goes the origin of the universe. What were you researching?"

"My life has been dedicated to one little bug. A virus, to be precise."

As we walked down the dingy corridors, footsteps echoing, I had a nagging feeling of something missing. At last I put my finger on it. "Where are the scientists, Vlad?"

"In Germany. The minute you have a doctorate they open the door. German science will soon be the best in Europe again and all with Russian brains. Except the Jews who go to Israel so they can go to California. Everyone is looking for a Jewish great-grandmother in the family. 30,000 scientists have left the country."

"Why don't you go?"

"I have offers. Do I want my girls to be Americans? What about my old folks?"

"You've still got the doorman and the cleaning lady."

"They would go too if they had the chance. We have some students and some old professors. They are lucky to earn fifty dollars a month. We have a double doc who makes pies in the afternoon for her mother to sell."

"How will you survive?"

"We try to make business for the Institute. We must make our knowledge pay for us. I do not make pies yet. I try to think how we can use this building."

"How about a baked potato restaurant? We'll call it Spuds and Bugs."

"Why not? We rent our basement to a *biznismyen* for his clothes from Vietnam."

My entrepreneurial mind was buzzing. Today's Special – Primal Soup.

Vladimir lived in the salubrious southwest, at the end of the red line. The apartment was light and airy. His beautiful wife was a physicist in another institute. Although we had never met, it was an emotional reunion, a sign that times had changed for the better since we brought letters from our Evil Empire to theirs. Their pretty daughters tried out their English and politely ran away to their bedroom to collapse into laughter at my Russian. A pedigree spaniel completed the household.

In Soviet days scientists were among the élite of society. They were respected, well paid, went to good schools and hospitals, enjoyed cruises and foreign junkets in the guise of conferences. I could have been visiting a professional middle-class family anywhere in Europe, even to the roast pork stuffed with prunes, a favourite among the intelligentzia of South London too. Over tea and cake we reverted to depression about the state of the former Soviet Union.

"People are saying Russia is besieged. We are undermined by foreign and domestic enemies. According to Marxist theory, Russia is ripe for revolution."

"Marx was often wrong. That was your problem in the first place. Think positive, Vladimir."

"I am a scientist. Positive thinking is a deliberate distortion of reality."

We eased the pain with another glass of Georgian red wine. Several Georgian reds lay claim to be Stalin's favourite. Thankfully this wasn't one of them. He liked medium sweet, which you may add to his catalogue of deficiencies.

The conversation segued seamlessly from politics to effluent. A few years ago the Institute was given a defence contract to develop technology for purifying air in closed environments. Human beings exude a cocktail of about eighty toxic substances. The scientists came up with the idea of using bacteria. The principle was not new: bacteria have been used to clean up water contamination since the beginning of the twentieth century. But cleaning air is a lot more difficult. They solved the problem with a device they called a Bioreactor, essentially a can full of specially selected bacteria that eat up the toxins. They were not told what it was for. It could have been for the Mir space station or, more likely, for nuclear submarines that spend months under water. Perhaps as you read this there are Bioreactors keeping the air sweet for submariners under the Arctic ice, what is left of it.

At the Institute they thought no more about it until one of the researchers met a director of a furniture factory. The fumes from the paint shop were outside the legal limit. The Institute scaled up the Bioreactor. It worked better than anyone had anticipated, clearing up over 95 per cent of the fumes. In the next four years they installed twenty Bioreactors in factories all over Russia.

"What keeps them in the can, Vladimir? Why don't they escape?"

"It is the only life they know. Outside they would perish. The Bioreactor is a living society, tiny little citizens going about their business. They find their place at the top or the bottom, the edge or the middle, and dedicate themselves to staying alive. They feed on carbon and oxygen and water like us. They are born and grow up and reproduce and die. They have different characters, different roles, different places in the hierarchy from the refined eaters on top down

to the hearty munchers at the bottom. They feed and defe-
cate, thrive in the right conditions, get listless if there is not
enough to eat, get fat and lazy if there is too much. It is a
good thing that they do not have the capability to ask why
they are doing this."

"If they did, would they behave any differently?"

"*You can get used to anything – even hell.* Tell me, John, is
there anything like our Bioreactor in the West?"

"Dunno, Vlad, I'll find out."

This was polite but insincere. The idea that Russians
could have environmental technology, what a joke! Everybody knew that Russians couldn't care less about the envi-
ronment. Territories the size of European countries were
wasteland. The quality of air and water in the cities was
lamentable. Russians put men in space, but the rest of their
technology was crude or copied from the West. In any case,
I had weightier matters on my mind.

"You don't know anyone who grows a good potato, do
you?"

"Dunno, John, I'll find out."

Vladimir's apartment was a haven of normality. However
busy the family were, I was always made to feel welcome. I was full of admiration for the way in which they
coped with their changing and uncertain world. Professors
in other institutes were making themselves rich by selling
patent rights or services to foreign companies. Western
patent agents came trawling, especially in defence-related
science, but Vladimir held fast to his personal integrity. In

one of the darker moments, when there was no more money for developing the Bioreactor, I offered him a thousand dollars to tide him over. He blanched.

"I am not like the others. I don't want to be like them."

"It's not a bribe, Vlad, it's an investment. We'll make it official."

"It is against the law. The Institute must surrender dollars and apply for a rouble grant."

"Take it unofficially."

"It is the slippery slope. *Gold is tested by man, man is tested by gold.*"

He invited me to see the Bioreactor in action at the All Union Shoe Works in an industrial suburb. Overwhelmed by economic conditions and Asian imports, only one floor of the six in the building was in operation. It was a big shed lit by grimy windows and harsh neon. Machines cut up plastic and fabrics into bits stuck together by the hands of men and women standing at long benches. They beavered in silence as we watched and relapsed into dilatoriness and chatter as we left. The shoes were for the kind of people who made them, a new pair at the beginning of winter, patched and glued to last the summer before they disintegrated beyond repair. They looked comfortably wide for my flat feet and I asked if they had a factory outlet. The director took one look at my brogues and thrust into my hands a pair of black 1970s stub toes from the end of the line. They fitted a treat and rounded off my Russian wardrobe.

"I wish you enjoyment, *tavarish*," said Vladimir, who was shod by Church's when he went to England for conferences.

★

The fumes from glue and hot plastic were sucked up by hoods and along ducting to the Bioreactor on the floor above. I tried hard to admire it, but all I could see was a bolted-together big blue can three metres high, shaped like the cylinder in the airing cupboard at home.

I met the Director of the Institute and two other laboratory heads to discuss ways of commercializing the Bioreactor in Western Europe. My advice, based on nothing but wishful thinking, was not to sell the technology outright but to license it in return for a share of the profits. The ideal partner would be strong in engineering and marketing but not have its own R&D. I speculated about what the agreement would contain and how the company would be structured. The upshot was that I was formally invited to investigate joint ventures with foreign companies. We signed a *protokol* appointing me as their agent.

That night, in Vladimir's kitchen, we worked out a proposal for me to present to engineering companies when I was back in Britain. There were facts and figures and drawings and reports on existing plants in Russia. I didn't like to say that the chances of a British company taking Russian environmental technology seriously were slim. There was a deep-seated aversion to innovations "not invented here". And there was a practical hurdle to cross.

"Vladimir, how do we get the bugs into England?"

"We freeze dry them like Nescafé. A bucket should be enough. We mix them with water and they come alive."

"They're still bacteria. How do we get a bucket of dry

bugs through customs?"

"It is only a small bucket. If you like we can make it smaller and send it through the mail."

"That's not the point. You can't just send bugs and germs across borders in your luggage or in the mail."

"Scientists do it all the time. This is how laboratories cooperate. You dip blotting paper into a test tube and put it in a envelope with a stamp. At the other end you take out the blotting paper and put it in a dish with some water. Very nice bacteria grow."

"But what if it's deadly germs like smallpox or anthrax?"

"The same. You will never stop these things at borders. You must stop them at the source."

"I don't believe it."

I decided to prove him wrong the next time I went back to London. We filled an old medicine bottle with flour and water and sealed it with the metal cap of a wine bottle. On his computer we printed a label marked with a skull and crossbones. In English and Russian we wrote "Danger. Russian Bacteria. Harmful if inhaled or swallowed." At Heathrow I went to the Red Channel. I took the bottle out of my briefcase and showed it to the Customs officer. He looked hard at the label.

"Wossis then?"

"Like it says. Live bacteria. From a Russian laboratory."

"How much is it werf?"

"Five thousand roubles."

"Ow much is that?"

"About seven pounds fifty."

"Gowon," he said crossly and waved me on.

"Sorry, officer, I want to declare this. It's Russian bacteria."

"Ow much did yew say it was werf?"

"About seven pounds fifty."

"Stop wasting my time."

"Are you sure it's not banned or anything?"

"Get out of here."

"I want to speak to your senior officer."

He gave a big sigh and went to fetch his superior. We went through the same dialogue again. I refused to go away until they had gone through all the manuals of Her Majesty's Customs, Board of Trade, Ministry of Health, Ministry of Agriculture, Fisheries and Food. They were right. There was nothing to prevent me taking my bottle into the country. In the next few days I phoned everyone I could think of who might be interested – the police, local authorities, Ministry of Defence, anybody. They all suggested I call the others.

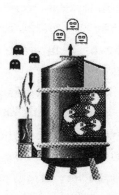

A sweet lie is better than a bitter truth

Vladimir was more conscientious in helping me with my potatoes than I was with his Bioreactor. He used his contacts at the Academy of Sciences to introduce me to a plant research institute in the town of Zelenograd, twenty-five miles northeast of Moscow. It was built in the 1950s as Russia's Silicon Valley and was a closed city. During the Soviet era you wouldn't find it on a map. It is now a commuter suburb of Moscow and easy to get to on the train.

I was picked up by my host, Professor Mishkin. We drove through the original town, an attractive place beside a river, and then through bleak and shabby high-rises to the institute on the edge of a collective farm. I imagine the idea was to transfer the research seamlessly into the fields, but there seemed an unbridgeable gap between the desolate fields and rundown buildings outside and the Eden inside.

Professor Mishkin was a very serious person. Solemn when we shook hands, as is conventional, she remained morose for the rest of our meeting. Perhaps her social skills were focused on talking to plants. Or she was uncomfortable showing off state secrets to a foreigner, spying on strategic vegetables. She showed me her lettuce. Tasked with inventing a device to grow fresh salad on the Mir space station, she had rigged up a slow-moving conveyor belt about two feet long inside a box equipped with a low-voltage red light. The conveyor was loaded with pellets of fibre soaked in hydroponic jelly, each holding a lettuce seed. The cosmonaut would simply switch on and in ten days young, fresh lettuce floated into the cosmos. Slapped in a sandwich with reconstituted salad cream, lovely.

Very interesting – but I was here for the potatoes. The reason Russian potatoes were misshapen leathery footballs was because the farmers could not afford proper seed. They used the leftovers from the previous year's crop. Through the generations these collected diseases and genetic defects from their earlier incarnations in the field. The modern way is to grow virgin potatoes from little green shoots that come out of the eyes. You weed out the imperfect tubers and grow another generation. You select these and then grow a third generation, which you sell to farmers. It takes three years. One of the tricks of the trade is knowing when to harvest them. The only way you know they are ready is to pull a plant up out of the soil and have a look, which is wasteful.

At Zelenograd they had perfected a different system. They took the tiniest little cutting from the tip of a green sprout, hardly visible to the naked eye. They put the cuttings into cabinets with artificial light and growing medium. The result was fragile little plantlets that they stuck into porous material over plastic gutters flowing with hydroponic fluid under artificial light. From these they grew the first generation of tubers. They were not at the mercy of the Russian winter and could grow all through the year. They had three crops, so the whole process took one year instead of three.

The real trick was installing everything two metres off the ground. They could turn off the fluid and lower the gutters, leaving the tubers dangling in the air. They harvested their spuds like fruit, plucking them overhead. They picked the ones that were ready, put back the guttering and left the rest for the next day. It was wonderful to see, so sensible and ludicrous. For 300 dollars cash down I signed a contract for enough seed to grow 5000 tons of lovely bakers. Now all I had to do was find the farmers to grow them. And the dry, ventilated sheds to store them. And the people to sort them and wash them and bag them.

Professor Mishkin said the European agency for the technology was available. We drafted a letter of intent. When I went back to the UK I called up the leading seed-potato growers in Scotland and Ireland and the Netherlands and described the system. They had a good laugh, so I didn't take on the agency. Pity. The Russians set up a company, grew to be world leaders and recently licensed McCain, the world's largest potato merchant. Another Big One slipped through the fingers.

Word got round the Union about the Western *expyert* at head office. I was invited to a collective farm, a *kolkhoz*, near Mtsensk, to advise them on how to regenerate their area with restaurants. I had no hesitation in accepting in the interests of seeing more of the country.

Mtsensk is 300 kilometres southwest of Moscow in the Oryol Oblast, four hours on the daytime express from Kurskaya station. No one else wanted to go, so for once I did not have a minder, trusted to look after myself between being put on the train by Natasha in Moscow and met at the other end by my host. From the train there wasn't much to note about the countryside. Flat and grassy bits alternated with birch forest and the occasional river.

Mtsensk will be known to opera lovers from *Lady Macbeth of Mtsensk* by Shostakovich, about a merchant's wife who sleeps with a farm hand, poisons her father-in-law and murders her husband. She is sentenced to Siberia, but kills herself on the way. When Stalin came to see it he ordered it suppressed on the grounds of sex and violence. Nevertheless, anyone who goes to Mtsensk hoping that the opera reflects the raciness of life there will be disappointed. The work is based on a story by Nikolai Leskov, who used Mtsensk as shorthand for quintessentially provincial, which, on the surface at least, it remains to this day. It would be like going to Rouen for excitement after reading *Madame Bovary*. For book lovers, the estate of the nineteenth-century writer Ivan Turgenev, famous for the novel *Fathers and Sons*, is 10 kilometres to the north. Unfortunately it was closed on the day I was there.

★

I was met off the train by Evgenia, my interpreter. She brought the apologies of the *kolkhoz* director, who had been called away on other business. She was about 50. Her hair, dyed pecan red, looked as if it had ten years at most before it gave up and fell out. I used to mock Western cosmetics, all that pseudo science and animal testing. Then I went to Eastern Europe, where women over 40 look like survivors of chemical warfare. Evgenia covered up most of the damage with a bright green knitted woolly hat, the same colour as her ankle-length padded coat. It was like walking round with a gooseberry promotion. She kept her outfit on and buttoned up all day, indoors or out, whatever the temperature. I kept telling her to take it off inside so she would feel the benefit, but she ignored me.

Evgenia introduced me to our driver, Vitaly, a broken reed of a man with the hollow chest and inward concentration of an emphysematic. He wasted none of his breath on conversation. He led us to a little white Lada and I was treated to a tour of the town. There wasn't much to see. In 1943 Oryol Oblast was part of the battlefield of Kursk, the biggest tank battle in history. Every building was flattened. In a hundred years or so tourists will come to gawp at the gems of Soviet architecture that replaced them, but meanwhile, since our tastes have not yet been formed in this direction, there is nothing to look at but monumentally dull public buildings and jerry-built apartment blocks.

We went to the Soviet-style Mtsensk Hotel for a Soviet-style lunch. Evgenia taught English to 12 year olds, which I agreed was an appropriate qualification for delivering a lec-

★

ture to an audience of aspiring *biznismyen*. Her small talk was out of an English conversation course. When we strayed from her script I had a horrible feeling that she didn't understand anything I was saying. She looked blank and jumped up and said she had to make a phone call. When she returned we went back to the module. I regretted not having a written text of my presentation to give her but, as I improvise around my overheads, it probably wouldn't have done her much good.

After lunch we drove through the autumnal countryside to the farm. A *kolkhoz* is a massive enterprise, a small town surrounded by agribusiness from production to processing. The employees live in multi-storey housing developments with all the amenities of a town – shops, cinema, hotel, sports facilities. We were in a sanatorium hotel on the edge of the surrounding forest. It was a pleasant enough place, all varnished wood and rough plaster. My audience of administrators were tired, middle-aged men in tired, middle-aged suits going through the motions, so I felt quite at home. Charged with reviving the fortunes of the farm with business initiatives, I was the foreign *expyert* who would tell them how to do it. Or rather I told Evgenia, who told them how to do it.

In the event I could have saved my breath on the first stage. My fears about her competence were fully justified. Her credibility as an interpreter depended on the audience not knowing English or the speaker not knowing Russian. I knew enough to realize that what she was telling them bore only an occasional resemblance to what I was saying. To test her I threw in whole sentences of gibberish. She steamed ahead with her own text without turning a desiccated hair. Lord knows where she got it, probably a hotchpotch of stuff from other *expyerts* she had worked for. The overheads, which were in Russian, kept us both going more or less in the right direction, but between these landmarks she beat her own path.

There was no harm done. Most of the audience weren't listening and those who were would have twisted and filtered and adapted my ideas to their Russian perceptions. Evgenia was just saving them the bother. The best I could do was pace around and wave my arms in the hope that brio would infect them with entrepreneurial enthusiasm. This had no apparent effect. To a man they looked stolidly down at the floor and asked no questions at the end. Their leader stood up, thanked me and shook my hand. They filed meekly out, pulling cigarette packets out of pockets.

I didn't have the heart to complain about the interpretation. Evgenia was desperate for the work. She had an unemployed husband and a student son to feed. The school had not paid its teachers for three months. Teachers subsisted on fees in kind brought in by the children – a loaf of bread, a bunch of onions, a jar of vegetables. I think she kept her coat on all day because it was the only decent thing she had to wear. I gave her ten dollars and she burst into tears. If my audience got the wrong end of the stick, so what? They wouldn't have known what to do with the right end.

I was surprised to be left to my own devices for the rest of the afternoon before Vitaly took me back for the evening train. The director had not delegated a minder. Evgenia was full of apologies. She had to go back to her school. The dinner ladies were baking pizza for the staff and if she wasn't there she wouldn't get her ration. I promised to stay quietly in the hotel lobby. There is a fine line between hospitality and surveillance and I felt unusually liberated.

As soon as everyone had gone I went out for a walk. It was a lovely, warm and sunny afternoon and I left my hat and coat behind. A footpath led from the back of the hotel across farmland to a forest about half a mile away. It was muddy from recent rain, but there was enough of a grass verge to keep my shoes dry. To my inexpert eye the uncultivated fields looked abandoned rather than deliberately fallow. They were covered in dense weeds and shoulder-high thistles. Hay had been cut but left uncollected in mounds. Abandoned sheds were missing windows and doors and roofs. The newest built were in the worst condition, from which I surmised that they had been looted before they were neglected.

The path continued into the forest, kept open by mushroom and berry hunters. I will leave you the chore of depicting for yourself a wood in autumn, with words like dappled, rich, warm, moist, ripe, rustle and so on. Put me in the picture, scuffing happily through the leaves until, as Raymond Chandler advises, when things slow down, bring in a man with a gun.

I don't know who was more surprised: me to see a man in camouflage toting a shotgun in a lonely Russian forest, or him to see a man in a pinstriped banker's suit, white shirt, stripy tie and loafers. As he had the gun, I bet my bowels turned to water before his. *When in doubt, bluff it out* is a motto that has stood me in good stead, so I did.

"*Zdravstvitye*," we said to each other as we approached. If this had been England we would have given each other a little nod and passed by like well-brought-up members of the Ramblers' Association. No such luck. He blocked the path, cradled his gun and looked me up and down, as I did him. I took comfort from the fact that he resembled a genuine hunter and not a psychopath on the loose. He wore a green felt hat with a little peak and dangling earflaps, green camouflage jacket and trousers tucked into lace-up paratrooper's boots, a loaded cartridge belt and a brown canvas game bag. The best thing was that his gun was broken and, as far as I could see, unloaded.

"*Sind Sie Deutsch?*" he asked.

"*Nyet. Anglichanin*," I replied, to his evident disappointment. However, I do speak reasonable German and could explain more fluently than in my Russian that I was a foreign *expyert* come to enlighten the *kolkhozniks* of the neighbourhood and not a fugitive bank manager.

"Come, my friend, let us pass the time of day together," he said and as he was the one with the gun, unloaded or not, I graciously accepted his invitation to step off the trail into a little clearing furnished with a convenient fallen log.

He was about my age, with nice brown unmurderous eyes. From his weather-beaten face he obviously spent a lot of time in the open. Fresh air and sunshine had done little

★

to cheer him up. His facial expressions and body language said glum, exceptionally so, even by Russian standards. But he seemed harmless, I hoped. He emptied his game bag onto the log between us – a heel of bread, a jar of pickled cucumbers, a greaseproof-paper parcel, a clasp knife, two small tin cups and an old-fashioned medicine bottle of ominously clear, brownish and slightly viscous liquid. He uncorked the bottle and filled the cups. I sniffed mine and was instantly transported to the moment in my childhood when we finally tracked down the smell in my bedroom to a dead mouse behind the skirting board.

"*Nazdarovye*," he said, "welcome to Mukhosransk."

"*Nazdarovye*, here's to Mukhosransk," and I downed the cup in one nose-clenching gulp.

"How do you like it?" he asked.

Easy-drinking firewater, full of fruity privet and deadly-nightshade flavours, aromatic on the nose with hints of last year's acorns followed by a pond-water palate and parrot-cage finish.

"Very nice. What is it?"

"*Samorgon*." Moonshine, as if I couldn't tell. He unwrapped the greaseproof parcel to reveal a thick slice of something white and buttery. He cut it into cubes and handed me one on the point of his knife. It was repulsive and delicious at the same time, like the fatty rind of insufficiently fried bacon. He broke off a chunk of bread to give me, followed by a gherkin.

"Very nice. What is it?"

"*Salo*. Good for the heart."

Had I known that *salo* is raw, salted pig fat I would have asked him in what way it was good for the heart, but fortunately I remained in ignorance.

"Do you work on the *kolkhoz*?" I asked.

"I am the director of the Park of Culture and Leisure City. Luna Park."

"Ah," was all I could say. I would have put him down as director of a crematorium sooner than an amusement park.

"Now is a quiet period."

"The winter."

"No. The last two years. Nobody comes. Most rides are closed. We have no money for spare parts. The Eisk factory only takes dollars. We have the roller coaster 'Panoramic View'. The passengers must haul the cars to the top themselves, but they are too lazy. Gyelter-Skyelter is open. It has no engine. All others are closed. Whirlwind, Ship's Boy, Little Birch."

"They sound really exciting."

"Yes. We would like investment from abroad. I have written to Mr Valt Dizneh. I am waiting for his reply. We have a very good location. Moscow four hours. Will you find English capitalists to give me money for this?"

"I'll talk to my people."

"Thank you."

I felt that he was saying all this because it was what he expected himself to say. His heart wasn't in it. He knew that his park was doomed and he didn't care. He was like Evgenia and my audience, going through the motions, their purpose in life sucked out of them. I tried to cheer him up.

★

"I'm sure things will get better. Russia is a great country."

"What do we do with her? We have tried serfdom. We have tried collectivism. Now we try anarchy. This is the Russian cycle. In the old days they said that anyone who rebelled against society was insane. They put them in mental hospitals. Now we opened the asylum doors and the madmen are running the country. Before we had apartments and heating and hot water and bread and vodka. Now we live in a madhouse where everyone has the same obsession – getting money. When I was a boy this was a field. They grew carrots and turnips. Now it is rabbits and mushrooms."

I know which I'd rather have, but I let it pass. Never contradict a man with a gun.

"You have plenty of time to hunt, then."

"The gun is my alibi. The only people who are allowed to walk alone are hunters and holy men. I have a simple life. I walk and breathe and eat and sleep and sometimes I shoot things, otherwise people would be suspicious. Anyway, it is good to kill once in a while. It is real. There is no illusion in the dead."

I began to get nervous again. If he reached for a cartridge on his belt it would be time to run like hell. I had no desire to be his reality check for the day. Looking back, I think my fears were unfounded. He was more likely to turn the gun on himself.

"Well, that was very nice," I said, brushing crumbs off my trousers. "I must go. Train to catch."

We stood up and shook hands in the sincere and meaningful way that you do when you know you will never see the other person again.

"I'll be in touch. About investors for your park."

"*A sweet lie is better than a bitter truth.* Thank you."

The sun was going down and a cool breeze blew up. I left him on his log staring at the ground in a gentle rain of falling leaves. For days afterwards people cracked up laughing when I said I'd been advising on restaurants in Mukhosransk. Then Flor explained that it is slang for the middle of nowhere, literally where flies go to shit.

Gather in the mushrooms

We wanted to import as little as possible and that included equipment for the restaurant. All except the oven. I was under strict instructions from Malcolm that only a Blodgett from Vermont would do. I called on Mashinimpex, suppliers of ovens to the catering trade. Their offices and showroom were in the suburb of Yasenevo, south of the city at the end of the Yellow Line near the MKAD, the Moscow ring road. It was a pleasant place, right next to Bitsevsky Park, 20 square kilometres of natural forest. Since 1972, when it moved from the Lubyanka, Yasenevo has been the home of the SRV, the Foreign Secret Service, equivalent to the CIA's Langley and MI6's Vauxhall Cross, otherwise known as Langley-on-Thames. A change from the days of Burgess, Maclean, Philby and Co. when the old HQ in Curzon Street was known as the London Lubyanka.

It was a pleasant afternoon. To clear my head of pre-heat times, BTUs, inlet pressures, core temperature probes and other mystifying terms of art, I went for a walk in the woods before getting the metro back to the centre. On the fringes there were mainly mothers and *babushkas* with babies, and several solitary old men with walking sticks wandering round in suits adorned with rows of medal ribbons as if they had got lost from a parade.

I walked aimlessly along the winding paths, enjoying the golden sun, luminous sky, ripe fruit and new mulch, happy to have the company of mushroom hunters. From the middle of summer to the first frost of winter you are rarely alone in a forest. Sit quietly on a log and sooner or later you will hear a shuffling and scuffling through the leaves, glimpse a plastic bag, a stooped figure. Mushroom picking is not social like berry picking. Berry picking is mindless, instinctive, you let the fingers do the work while you chat or daydream. Mushroom picking is silent and solitary, even in company. You have to concentrate because they are not easy to spot. It is said that women are better at it than men because they have a more developed sense of shape and colour. Then comes the business of drying or salting or pickling at home for the winter. There are some classic dishes using fresh mushrooms, mainly in pies and soups, but most are preserved. Every family has its own mysteries and recipes.

As does every language, Russian has picturesque names for mushrooms: Caesar's, the buttery, the Polish, the little fox, the little goat, the little pig, the stinky fly killer. The finest are the "whites", the fragrant, meaty boletus that we know as cep or porcini. These have nothing to do with the Anglo-Saxon white mushrooms, the industrial variety

★

otherwise known as champignons or button mushrooms, which in pizzas, pies and most other recipes can be substituted with slivers of polystyrene from the packaging they came in. Russian mushrooms, preserved or fresh, bear so little resemblance to our bland supermarket fungi, even the fancy ones, that I only think of them by their Russian name, *greebi*.

Greebi are a way of life, a part of Russian folklore and proverbs. Good people in folk tales are pictured with whites, bad people with toadstools. When Pushkin or Tolstoy wanted to show a character was a true Russian he had them prefer mushrooms to fancy foreign food. *Anna Karenina* is full of mushroom and mushroom-picking imagery. Mushrooms signify nature and vitality and hope for the future. For the exiled Nabokov, mushrooming is a symbol of his lost Motherland. Lenin is reputed to have been a keen mushroomer. One rainy day, so the myth goes, he was hurrying to the station when he spotted a clump of whites and stopped to collect them, in spite of the rain, the train and his wife's protestations. Ahh, man of the people. Children learn to walk to a rhyme promising they will go mushroom hunting when they can. When I got excited about some hare-brained idea, Misha shut me up with *If mushrooms grew in your mouth, it wouldn't be a mouth but a kitchen garden.* My favourite, when we had to arselick some *apparatchik* for a favour, was *You can't pick a mushroom without bowing.*

Musing on such things, I didn't notice how late it had become. The sun sank below the tree tops. Birds launched into their bedtime chorus. A chill evening breeze rattled the leaves. I was at a crosspaths and had no idea which of the four to take. I looked round for a walker or a mushroomer, but everyone else had gone home. Had I known then about the Bitsevsky Park Murderer, Russia's most prolific serial killer, I would not have been so keen to ask directions. He confessed to 69 murders, starting his spree about a year before my little adventure. He preyed on solitary people, creeping up from behind and bopping them on the head.

I didn't have a map, but I knew that north would take me further into the forest with about ten miles of wooded hills and the Bitsa River before I came to the Garden ring road. To the east was the suburb of Chertanovo, which had no metro station. South was less good as I would come to the MKAD, Moscow's M25. Best was west, back to Yasenevo and the metro stations. But which way was west? The sun had gone so there was no fiddly Boy Scout stuff to be done with a watch as a compass. There were no stars yet and in any case the foliage overhead would prevent a decent sight-ing. Aha! Boys' lost-in-the-wilderness adventure stories to the rescue. *Moss grows only on the north side of tree trunks.* So by keeping the moss on my left I would face west and get back to the station. That was the theory and in the absence of any other, it would have to do.

In practice it was less perfect. Some trees had no moss at all. Some had moss on all sides. Some had moss on the opposite side to their immediate neighbours. To make it worse, the paths were winding so you often turned counter-mosswise, then back again. But I pressed on, hoping the anomalies would cancel out and happily oblivious of the advice in serious survival guides that "it is a fallacy that moss only grows on the north side of trees. In dense woodland this method is especially unreliable." As a method of navigation it was as much use as forecasting the weather from whether the cows are lying down. But, as in many other situations in life, truth brings despair and fallacy brings hope, so I pressed on through the gathering darkness.

Mine is the last generation to whistle, which I did to keep my spirits up. I wasn't really worried. It was getting cold, but I wouldn't freeze to death. Every good hike has a "God get me out of here and I'll never do this again" moment, otherwise it's just a ramble. When you have the right gear like a compass and a map, getting lost is fun. Getting out of a fog or a forest by dead reckoning is an exciting challenge. I would love the sport of orienteering if it wasn't for the running. There is a deeply primitive satisfaction in navigation that we inherit from our hunter-gatherer past and that the GPS and the mobile phone have ruined for ever.

It had been dark for an hour and I was feeling my way uphill when I heard the sound of thunder. I stopped whistling and groped around for a waterproof bush to shelter under for the night, until I realized it was the noise of traffic. Hope flared. I came to the top of the rise and saw headlights strobing through the trees. So much for moss – I had come south to the MKAD. It took another half an hour of inching through the undergrowth before I staggered out of the trees into what looked like bonfire night. A score of articulated trucks were parked in a long lay-by carved out of the forest. Men stood round a massive brazier ten feet long and three feet wide or sat on logs around a camp fire.

I patted my hair and brushed twigs off my sports jacket and twills and took my tie off, so as not to look too much of a berk. Grimy, scratched and bedraggled, I sauntered to the fire, hands in pockets, a chap out for an evening stroll. When I felt the heat I realized how cold I was, which gave me courage to join the party. Stocky Russians with a leavening of Finns and Caucasians, Mongols and Tatars. Far from home, they had the brawny arms, spreading buttocks and low-slung bellies of truck drivers everywhere. They were drinking from litre jam jars refilled from metal jerry cans. They glanced at me for a moment and carried on eating and talking in *mat*, the obscene lingua franca of men.

They were having a barbecue. Lumps of meat were impaled on long spikes stuck into the ground and leaning at 45 degrees over the flames. These were no dainty cubes of meat but bloody chunks the size of a small joint. Tough meat for tough men – the Russian truck driver is no sissy. The long-distance ones travel in pairs, one to drive and one to ride shotgun, or rather Kalashnikov.

A shaggy, pockmarked man was in charge. Sweating in wife-beater and jeans, he turned the meat and took it off the spikes when it was done. He hacked off replenishments with an axe from a carcase lying on the grass, which I trusted had fallen off the back of a lorry and not been run over by one. Like most minorities, I thought myself more interesting than the majority did and felt obliged to explain to the chef how I had got there, laying the English accent on thick.

"You want to eat?" was all he was interested in. "Five hundred roubles." I gave him a dollar and received in return a jam jar of piss-coloured liquid and a chunk of meat on a hunk of black bread on a bit of newspaper. I took this primitive takeaway to a vacant packing case among other patrons round the fire. I did not recognize the beverage. It was certainly fizzy home brew, but of what it was hard to say. It might have been beer or *kvas* or something else entirely. The sour metallic taste could have come from the ingredients or foul-tasting Moscow water. Although it tasted nasty, it was very nice. There should be a word in gastronomy equivalent to the French *jolie-laide*, which describes a woman who is ugly yet attractive. Guinness, pumpkin pie and haggis are inherently disgusting but delicious. "An acquired taste" is too poncey. Nice-nasty will have to do.

Under the stars, in the flickering firelight, search-lit by the headlights of thundering rigs, gnawing at a charred chunk of roadkill, slugging down an unidentified nice-nasty beverage, I felt brave and lucky, like a lone wanderer on the steppe, stumbling across a nomad encampment. One of my dining companions, a tough little man with a bald head and hairy knuckles, took a swig of his jar, wiped his greasy fingers in his armpits and slapped his palms on his knees.

"Ho, Englishman! Who am I?" he bellowed over the noise of the traffic. "Famous Englishman!" He rolled his eyes and contorted his mouth into a leer and wriggled his fingers as if he was threatening to tickle a toddler. The others chortled and pointed and stamped their feet at the impersonation, but I was stumped. What Englishman could he possibly know?

"Vinston Tzertzill?" I hazarded.

"*Nyet*," they roared.

"Tzemz Bornd?"

"*Nyet*," they roared. The little man stood up and ran to and fro, knees bent, rolling his eyes and wiggling his fingers. The others laughed and clapped their hands and chanted "*aketizak aketizak*". Thank God I twigged at last.

"Benny Kheell!"

"*Da*," they roared. My jam jar was refilled, I was clapped on the back, I basked in reflected comic glory. This was my cue. The song "Gather in the Mushrooms", immortalized by Benny Hill, is my party piece for Christmas, birthdays, every family singsong. My children, nephews and niece loathe it and shout me down, so it always fills me with warm feelings of nostalgia, especially when I am alone and far away.

"Gather in the mushrooms, put them in a pot,
Pop 'em in the oven an' serve 'em piping ho-ot."

I treated them only to the chorus, as my Russian was not up to translating the subtlety of the verses. I explained that mushrooms was the theme and substituted *greebi* in the

★

lyric. They were ecstatic. Unlike my family, they demanded encores. The impersonator snuggled up to me on my packing case and demanded private tuition. They sang other songs, which I did not recognize but were evidently of the same genre. Happy to have made a contribution I nibbled what I could of my food, threw the rest behind me into the bushes and, in a lull in the singing, announced it was time for me to go. One of the drivers kindly offered to take me the mile or so along the ring road to the metro station. As I climbed into his rig I heard the impersonator's fruity baritone.

> *Gyedder in de greebi, pootem inner port*
> *Poppem inna orven en sierem paipin hort*

Since the dawn of civilization culture has spread along trade routes. Who knows how far *Gyedder in de Greebi* has spread along the motorways through Russian-speaking lands, how many generations will hand it down? From tiny spores great mushrooms grow. It's nice to give something back.

If you don't grease you don't travel

The Mayor of Moscow, Yuri Luzhkov, announced that only the Cyrillic alphabet was to be used on public signs and logos. McDonald's had to become МАКДОНАЛДС and Pizza Hut ПИЦЦА ХАТ. And Jackets? ДЖЭКЭТС. We were relying on foreigners to fuel our launch. McDonald's and Pizza Hut had recognizable logos, but Jackets? How would a foreigner ever recognize ДЖЭКЭТС? How would they know it was Western? And what would entice affluent Russians to taste a bit of England in a place that looked like it was named after a factory town in the Urals?

Misha, who was on a visit from Rome, Oleg and I sat round our world headquarters in the bedroom plunged into gloom. Like 1920s Bolsheviks we bemoaned Russian chauvinism, bourgeois nationalism, the death of internationalism. What is to be done? Who is to blame?

Every problem is an opportunity. Because Jackets did not have a brand presence outside South London, we were not shackled by it. There was nothing to stop us changing to a euphonious and compelling name that would appeal to both Russians and foreigners. But what? Look carefully at the Russian names above. Some letters you would have no idea how to pronounce unless you deduced them from the context. Ж for example, or Л or Ц. Others look familiar but are deceptive: Russian H is our *n*, C is *s* and X is *h*. As any stamp collector will tell you, the Russian for USSR is CCCP – three *s* words followed by an *r*. If you can bear to look at those junk-food names again without feeling nauseous, you will see five letters that look the same and sound the same in Cyrillic and Roman.

"AKMOT," I shouted. "That's our answer!"

"AKMOT? Is this a name for a restaurant? It does not sound too tasty to me." In Russian it is pronounced AKMORT, which is even more sinister.

"It is so meaningful. So symbolic. It's what we have in common, the bridge between two languages, two cultures. In these five letters is the meeting of East and West…"

"We are selling potatoes, not world peace."

"All we have to do is make up a name with these letters and put it in lights."

After some discussion, and bowing to the wisdom of a Western marketing expert and entrepreneurial consultant, they came round to the idea, which, like many such ideas, was more exciting in concept than in practice. We soon exhausted the anagrammatical possibilities of using each letter only once. In theory there are 120 combinations of five letters but only 28 were pronounceable. None of them was very catchy. "Let's go out for a MOKTA" didn't sound appetizing in Russian or in English. We tried using any four of the five letters, which added 32 potential names, all of which sounded more like acronyms for trade unions than a lifestyle choice. We relaxed the rules again to allow one letter to be repeated. This was more promising, producing words like TATO, which got closer but meant nothing in Russian. For potato they use the German word, *Kartoffel*. Oleg, who was of a mathematical bent, calculated that there were 720 possibilities, minus the unpronounceable. We each took a different starting letter and a piece of paper and laboured over the various combinations. Misha favoured KAKA, which summed up his opinion of the whole project.

Olga called us to the samovar in the kitchen. We explained what we were doing as she passed round the glasses.

"There must be people all over Moscow doing what you are," she said.

I don't remember who first had the brainwave. It may have been a collective inspiration, synapses firing in unison to produce a cerebral tsunami. All we had to do was come up with the best names, register them at City Hall as our own, and wait for international companies to come crawling to buy them off us. It was the sort of thing people do with internet domain names and car number plates. We had to move fast. It was such a great idea that we would surely have competition.

"Do you know how to register the names?" asked Olga, ever practical.

"I suppose we go to City Hall and ask. There must be a procedure," I said.

★

How they laughed. When you need to do anything legal or official the first thought is not "Where do I go?" or "What time do they open?" or "Where do I get the forms?" but "Who do I know there?"

"*Znachet*," said Misha, "we will find someone to bribe."

Trembling with entrepreneurial fever, we went back to work. We did not underestimate the challenge. If we allowed two letters to be repeated the permutations were even more promising with words like TOMATO, but there were 5760 of them. Allow three letters to be repeated and you get French-sounding brands like TAMTAM and MAK-MAK. To find all of them you would have to trawl through more than 45,000 combinations. With pencil and paper it would take us weeks. Undaunted, Oleg said we should write a computer program.

Russian computers were inferior to American and Japanese. To compensate for this, and because their maths education is better than ours, Russians are leaders in software. So it was child's play for Oleg to sit down at the computer to knock off a program that would permutate and sift AKMOT according to our rules. As one who has sympathy with those who hunt for the "any" key on the keyboard, I went into the kitchen to watch television with Olga while she sewed French labels into Bangladeshi sweaters.

"You work very hard."

"We have to pay bills. Next week I go to Dubai for the first time."

"You're a shuttler! Well done! What happened to your boss?"

"She was killed. She cheated her roof." Roof is slang for protection by the mafia from the mafia.

"Aren't you frightened?"

"I must do it. Somebody must make money."

"Oleg works hard."

"He dreams of Spain. Misha makes him work."

"They have big plans."

"Yes, big plans. Men have the best ideas. Men control everything. *Women's path is from the stove to the door.*" She smiled and poured tea.

Less than an hour later the printer began to stutter dense paragraphs of gibberish.

"Oleg! *You could shoe a flea!*"

Like excited cryptographers we chanted out the names that took our fancy as they rose from the rollers. The thrill wore off by the second page. It was obvious that even after the computer had done its first cull of the unpronounce-able, there would be thousands of names, hundreds of pages. I would have given up the whole idea and gone home to bed, but I was with Russians. Although they didn't espe-cially believe in the idea, now they had started they would stick to it with dogged tenacity. Oleg broke open a fresh ream of paper – coarse, brownish, unbleached stuff with wood shavings embedded in it that today would be so envi-ronmentally correct but then seemed more appropriate to an outside toilet than the IT hub of a nascent multina-tional. Olga refilled the samovar, made a plate of *kolbasa* sandwiches and went to bed on the sofa in the living room. Oleg and Misha sat up on the bed and I took the chair. We shared out the sheets as they emerged and crossed out names, at first with much deliberation and then more cursorily. We just about kept up with the printer. And still they came, surely more trade marks than there were companies in those early days of the free market.

The night wore on. From time to time lids grew heavy, a pen slipped from the fingers, a head dropped. If we didn't snort into wakefulness, one of the others would poke us in the ribs. We stuck to our task like Stalin's commissars, purging names until dawn. Our work was not over when the printer at last fell silent. We swapped our sheaves and went through them again, me crossing out their Russian suggestions and they deleting my English candidates. When Olga got up she found us in the kitchen, fast asleep, our heads on the table. But we had our list. Two hundred plump and juicy names ready for the signwriters and the neon-lighters. AMMO and MAMA, MOOMOO and MOKKA, KOMA and KOKO. Now all we had to do was register them and wait for the money to roll in. This was a Big One.

L uck was with us. Finding someone in City Hall was easy. I was walking along Tverskaya, suited up with white shirt and naff tie covered in currency symbols, on my way back from the Central Bank where I had discussed agricultural finance with a deputy director, who knew even less than I did. 13 Tverskaya is City Hall, a great pink-brick block of a building with two tiers of classical columns stuck on the front. Some of my friends are rude about it but, coming from Birmingham where we have the Parthenon at the top of New Street, I am partial to neoclassical kitsch. At the main door of the building a trio of men in the same uniform as me were waggling bits of paper at the bored policeman in his kiosk. Quite apart from our registration project I was curious for a peek inside the building, so I tagged on behind as he waved us through into the cavernous vestibule, where a buxom false-redhead dressed like a massage-parlour receptionist was waiting for us – or rather, as I imagine a massage-parlour receptionist would be dressed. She took us up in the lift to the official reception rooms on the second floor.

Too late to turn back, I stood in line with the other suits and waited to be ejected by the bouncer with the guest list. I had stumbled into a reception for foreign bankers. Luzhkov was schmoozing them for municipal finance. They had spent the day listening to presentations and this was their reward. It was my naff tie that did it. I was waved through into a ballroom, all glossy parquet and gilt and mirrors and violent crimson wallpaper. In the far corner a youthful string trio dressed for the nineteenth century sawed away at Rimsky-Korsakov, although judiciously avoiding the "Flight of the Bumblebee". I joined thirty or so clones mingling with our hosts around a circular buffet table and its handsome bowl of truly excellent caviar.

I have been to enough bankers' dos around the world to know how to blend in. The secret is to look serious, say little and respond to any comment with "Hmm, the dollar." Then people think you are powerful and burdened with financial secrets. I did not feel bad about gate crashing,

★

since several of the others seemed as flaky as I was and a couple were definitely lightweights, the way they nattered on about bond rates and yields, trying to impress.

These days the Russians would have been indistinguishable from the rest of us, unless it was by the superiority of their tailoring. Then, most men over 30 remained sartorially Soviet in light grey suits, shiny shirts and pastel shoes. An exception was Stepan Gavrilovich, who generously heaped my plate with second helpings of the Caspian's finest. He sported an aspirational Marks & Spencer-style double-vented pinstripe complete with matching tie and hankie. He had the Mediterranean looks of a Georgian and was young enough to think he needed to tint his hair grey at the temples. He spoke the excellent English taught in Russia, finished off by Voice of America.

Nervous about being rumbled, I went on the conversational offensive and asked what he did. He said that he was an adviser and asked what I did. I said I was an adviser. I could not avoid the business-card ritual. He crossed out the telephone number on his and wrote in a new one. Otherwise it asserted that he was Head of the Development Section in the mayor's office. We were saved from further exploration of our credentials by the grand entrance of Mayor Luzhkov and his entourage.

Since 1992 Yuri Luzhkov has run Moscow like a Tsarist Governor General. He makes his own laws. If he doesn't like those of the national parliament and courts, he ignores them. City Hall is an entrepreneurial investor with a stake in every real-estate, industrial and media business in

Moscow. It has been the prime mover behind the renovation, restructuring and rebuilding of the city. Many have made fortunes by working with it, not least the richest woman in Russia, who happens to be Luzhkov's wife Yelena. Cronyism and corruption are rife, from the top down to the humblest restaurant inspector.

At the same time, economic growth and standard of living outstrip the rest of Russia. Ailing privatized industries like the ZIL auto plant have been renationalized and revitalized. Municipal services have been improved, low-cost housing built and pensions restored. The combination of free-market economics, cronyism, directiveness and demagoguery smacks more of Tammany Hall than any Russian precedent. Despite, or perhaps because of, all this, Luzhkov has been re-elected three times and is the longest-serving democratically elected politician in Russia. He founded the Fatherland party and was in the running for President until Yeltsin anointed Vladimir Putin as his successor.

Charisma is an overused word for a rare quality, but Luzhkov has it. He is little and bald, but his presence filled the room, as it has filled the city for the past fifteen years. He was bright and energetic with a charming smile that you felt could turn into a glower in an instant. He glad-handed the room, starting with me.

"Bank?" he asked. He had the uncanny ability of charismatic short men to give the impression that they are looking down on you. I chickened out of saying "Jackets Baked Potatoes".

"Private placements?" I stuttered, and this was translated by a minder.

"Is this good for Moscow?"

"Hmm, the dollar." He shook my hand, shrunk back to size and moved on. Stepan, who had left me to face the great man alone, slipped back to my side and refilled my glass with the excellent vodka.

"Impressive person," I said, star-struck.

"He does not drink and he does not smoke," said Stepan, lighting up a Marlboro. "Can you trust such a Russian?" He smiled and I didn't know whether to take him seriously. "Now, let us discuss what I can do for you."

"Well, as it happens…"

He thought our scheme was brilliant. He said such innovative thinking was just what Moscow needed. Better still, he knew just the right person in City Hall. We should discuss it further. He had a very crowded agenda, but a lunch the day after tomorrow had been cancelled. He suggested the Exchange American steakhouse at the new Radisson Hotel. The Exchange was way out of my budget, but surely just one of our new trade marks was worth more than a foreign-currency lunch. I was lucky to get a table. Russian restaurants still clung to traditional values of terrible food and worse service and there were few Western establishments.

The Radisson opened in 1991 on the far bank of the Moskva river near the Kiev railway station. There was a good view of the wedding-cake Stalinism of the Ministry of Foreign Affairs and, further downstream, the radiator-grille façade of the Russian parliament, the White House. Not that the Radisson was better. It looked like a multi-storey car park with windows. Although I was only ten minutes late, Stepan was waiting for me in the lobby. Punctuality is not one of the many Russian virtues, from which I deduced either that he was keen or that he had got the time wrong. I dislike tipping before you sit down, or indeed any time, so the *maître d'* showed us to what I immediately judged was the worst table in the room, and I should know, I am an *habitué*. But Stepan was not daunted. He rubbed his hands and flicked out his cuffs, looked round at our fellow suits and admired the orange napkins origamied into scallops.

The waiter brought menus. I gulped at the prices and Stepan slavered over the choices. I had a mixed salad and a hamburger. He had Maine lobster and a fifty-dollar *filet mignon*. We had Margaritas while the white cooled and the red breathed.

"You see, John, how Russia changes. We do not change very often but when we do, kabam."

He smiled, showing off a gold canine. I have gold teeth too and am embarrassed by them, but Stepan flashed his, a sign of affluence in a country where you still saw false teeth made of steel.

"Why is it like that? Why do things carry on and on and then suddenly crack apart?" I asked.

"For you changing is always for the better. For us changing is always for the worse. When things are bad we think not 'How can we make it better?' but 'Let's do nothing in case we make it worse.'"

"Pessimism."

"Not pessimism, John, experience. You see, with you change comes from the bottom, from the people. With us change comes from the top. It is imposed on us. Like Gorbachev's. The people did not ask for them."

"Is that why you all hate him?"

"You know the joke about the old British colony that decides to change from driving on the left to driving on the right? So people will get used to the idea, they decree that cars will start immediately, trucks next week and buses the week after. This was Gorbachev. You cannot be half a virgin. You cannot have half a revolution. His *Perestroika* made wreckage and confusion. There were food queues in the cities and food rotting on the farms. He wanted multi-party democracy with the Communist Party in charge. The Republics were to be independent as long as they took orders from the Kremlin. Nuclear disarmament with the Americans went ahead, but who did the weapons belong to? Russia? Ukraine? Belarus? The Baltic states wanted independence, so why not Chechnya? And if Chechnya why not Siberia? It was a big mess."

The first course came. Stepan relished his lobster while I picked at my salad, wishing I hadn't been so stingy. I tasted the wine, a Chablis, which was excellent – and so it should have been at the price.

"Surely the biggest changes in Russia have come from people in the street?"

"Mobs change nothing. They riot when things become intolerable. They riot to resist change."

I nodded to the White House, which we might have been able to see from a better table.

"This mob of yours saved the day at the White House." This was after the attempted coup against Gorbachev when Yeltsin bravely stood on a tank.

"Ah, the White House. That was a triumph. We stopped the tanks, didn't we?"

"Were you there?"

"Of course. Three days at the barricades. Democracy and freedom, John. Let's drink to that."

At least 100,000 people had been at the White House on those fateful August days. Many more claimed they had been.

The main course came. I tasted the red, a Côtes du Rhône, which was also excellent. The hamburger was a hamburger. Stepan savoured the steak, relishing every mouthful with half-closed eyes. The main course was cleared away and we reached for the toothpicks. While Stepan impersonated a man giving himself a root canal, I explained our scheme in detail. His job was to get the business names registered at City Hall.

"John, why must we register the names?"

"So we have something to sell. If not, the companies can simply go and register their own names without us."

"But they will do that anyway."

"Not if we have registered them first."

"This means nothing. The companies will pay a bribe."

"Surely it's easier to pay us. In any case we will take them to court."

"What court? A tennis court?" He laughed. "Do not look so miserable, John. I am joking. It is a wonderful idea. *We will not be millionaires but we will have enough to eat.*"

I thought we'd had enough to eat already. The waiter came and Stepan chose a confection of meringues and expensive out-of-season fruits and fresh Irish cream and Kahlua. I settled for a lemon sorbet. Not being a brandy drinker, since it gives me hot flushes, I let him order a Courvoisier Napoleon. Fortunately I had remembered to bring along a couple of tubes of Romeo y Julietas from my stash and waved away the flunkey with the humidor before Stepan noticed him. I took out the envelope with the sheets of names and handed them over.

"Oh, good names. These are very good names." He looked at me over his snifter.

"How much will it cost to register them?"

"Nothing. Five roubles. Ten roubles. Twenty roubles. Give me five thousand roubles for the formalities." This was about twenty dollars. Didn't sound too bad. Compared with lunch, anyway.

"And we have to give something to the clerks," he said.

"How much do you think?"

"A thousand dollars."

"What! How much?"

"*If you don't grease you don't travel.* They have to eat too."

"But not in here. A clerk doesn't earn that in a year."

"There is the director and the supervisor and the clerk and the checker."

"I don't have that much on me."

"How much do you have?"

"Five hundred dollars. Less the tip here."

"I will start with that. Give it to me. Don't worry, John. You will have it all back in two weeks. We make a very good partnership. I have many contacts in the city and you have so many wonderful ideas. *The wolf of Tambov is your comrade.* I am a poor Russian, an old Communist. We did not believe all those things we were told, but what choice did we have? We do not know the modern world. We do not know how to seize the future. You must help us, John, with your experience and your intelligence and your education. We have so much to learn, we owe you so much."

I had a lump in my throat by the time he finished. It felt great to be making a difference. I emptied my wallet to Stepan in a haze of good feeling, good wine and good tobacco. We strolled back to Kievskaya station making plans for our next venture and took the Circle Line in different directions.

While ICBM waited to hear that Stepan had successfully registered the names, we prepared the marketing campaign. I drafted a press release for the foreign-language media and leaflets for the commercial sections of the main embassies and the business centres of the big hotels. At the end of the week I phoned Stepan, who told me that he had everything in hand. We were on an inside track, so it would not take the months or years it would normally, but the wheels of bureaucracy still ground slowly, even when liberally greased. He suggested I call again in two weeks. Meanwhile Oleg was keen to get our campaign going right

★

away. I insisted that as we would be dealing with Western companies, which were meticulous about such things, we must have the registrations properly signed and stamped before we started selling them.

Two weeks later I called Stepan. "Not here," said a man's voice and the phone went dead before I could reply. I wasn't concerned since Russian telephone manners are typically abrupt, especially in large organizations. If you are quick, you may be able to ask when the person will be back before the phone is put down, to which the standard reply is "in an hour". Only the tyro will take comfort from this and call back in an hour. It is an empty formula. The habits of secrecy acquired over decades of suspicion and surveillance die hard. You rarely tell anyone else where you are going or what you are up to; even if you did, they would not tell a stranger. This includes the secretary. It would be gross impertinence if she asked to see her boss's diary.

Alarm bells started to ring, as yet faintly, when I got the same answer twice more. I consoled myself with the thought that he had moved office or fallen ill. But why didn't he call me? There was nothing for it but to go and see him in City Hall. My heart was in my mouth when I asked for him at reception. I was very relieved when the guard looked up his name in a book and phoned his office.

"He will be down in a minute."

I paced up and down the lobby under its enormous chandelier hoping I had not made some terrible *faux pas* by chasing him. Russians can be touchy if you doubt their

167

loyalty. A little grey-haired man in his 60s in a tired grey sports jacket and knackered grey trousers came up to me.

"Mr Mole? How can I help you?"

I will gloss over the next half hour. Look up "emotion" in a thesaurus and you will get an idea of what I went through, from anger to vengefulness and all the words in between. The business card was the clincher. The genuine Stepan Gavrilovich showed me a card case full of them with the telephone numbers undeleted. He did not recognize my description of the imposter. To his knowledge there was no Registry of Business Names at City Hall. He advised me to try the Economics Ministry.

There was only one consolation. Over the coming months many new companies and shops put their names up in lights, but they used none of our selection. The Farmers' Union thought it a bad idea to have a Russian-sounding name for our restaurant and that we should stick with Jackets. I kept one of the names for myself, TAMKO. I went to the railway station and printed up some business cards in the DIY machine for my own use.

The Czar of Cheese

I had my Mozzarella Big One in a cowshed to the accompaniment of syrupy strings playing ABBA's *Greatest Hits* and the sweet smell of manure. They went well together.

By the spring your average Russian cow is a pathetic creature. She staggers out of the cowshed where she has been incarcerated since the first big snow of the previous November. When the temperature drops the windows are boarded up and felted over. The farmer breaks the ice on her water every morning. He gives her frozen hay to eat and whatever roots he doesn't need for himself. She stands on a slatted platform so her dung can go through to the earth floor to freeze – straw is too precious to waste. Her milk goes by Christmas. She may be alone, she may have companions, it depends how much fodder the farmer has managed to hoard for the winter.

When the snow starts to melt and the sun noons over the tree line and the air is filled with the elfish music of tinkling ice, the farmer opens the door and leaves the cow to come out into the light in her own good time. Shuffling and staggering, she emerges from the dark and the stench. Exhausted by the effort, she leans against a fence or a wall and waits for food, slack bellied, hollow sided, head hanging, ribs and haunch-bones too big for her body.

In winter the cows stopped producing milk because there wasn't enough food, in summer it went off quickly and many farms didn't have cooling facilities. It was unsurprising that fresh milk was hard to find. At the Irish House supermarket I bought Finnish milk in clear plastic bags. Most Russian milk went for cheese and ice cream and sour cream and other processed products. The creams and wheys and curds were nice enough, but you didn't linger over the cheese counter. The choice was yellow cheese or smoked yellow cheese.

I attended the annual congress of the Farmers' Union in the old Communist Party congress hall. Two thousand peasants from all over Russia under a massive Union flag, Eisenstein faces with hollow cheeks and bushy spade beards. I hadn't seen suits like it since Sunday mass in Mayo. During the speeches I sat next to a Swede called Klang who had come to the aid of the Russian dairy industry with a model dairy farm in Solnechnogorsk, northwest of Moscow, funded by the Swedish farmers' union. He had been a potato farmer in his youth and his Russian neighbour grew potatoes, so we had lots to talk about. I invited myself to his farm to discuss supplies for Jackets. I also wanted to visit Shakhmatovo, the country estate of Alexander Blok, a famous Symbolist poet caught up in the October Revolution.

Natasha drove me in her Niva. She was keen to go because news was seeping out that four years ago three

★

dead aliens from a crashed UFO had been taken to a secret research facility near Solnechnogorsk. She was meeting fellow Astralists in town to investigate. She was secretive about how they planned to locate the research facility, but I think it involved vibrations and telepathy and crystals. I can't remember what I said, if anything, I probably just laughed, but it was enough to put her in a huff. She didn't speak the whole trip.

There was slush on the road and the washer didn't work, so every ten miles Natasha had to pull over by a patch of cleanish snow and scatter it over the windscreen before she could use the wipers. For nine and a half miles it was like driving through brown fog. She dropped me at the rendez-vous with Klang at the turnoff from the motorway to the city and drove off in search of alien death.

The farm was on a gentle hill with views of rolling hills and forests and the distant lakeside city and a nearby state-owned dairy plant. Klang was a southern Swede, small and dark and with no trace of the singsong intonation that caricatures his nation. He had left his family in Sweden, as his children were of school age, and lived alone in a bare little bungalow decorated with bits of yellow and blue Swedery and marquetry portraits of cows from kits, which was his hobby.

He introduced me to his neighbour, who was keen to show me his potatoes. As I had come to expect, they were the size of large pebbles. But he had a handsome ventilated barn to keep them in, which I thought might come in useful.

Klang took me on a tour of his cowsheds. He had about fifty animals. Plump and contented, they lived in a bovine palace. No amenity had been spared, including piped music, warmed water, infra-red heaters, daylight-simulation bulbs, *en suite* milking facilities and discreet excretory arrangements. As well as the sweetest hay they had all kinds of grain and silage, seasoned with vitamins, minerals, probiotics, antibiotics and all the other desirable condiments for the modern cow. The end product was the finest milk in Russia.

I ummed and ahhed and dug deep for what I hoped were farmerly questions like whether he knew the cows by name and what their favourite music was. Inspired, I then asked about the breed. All he needed to tell me was that they were a cross between Swedish Red-and-White and Russian Red-and-White, combining Scandinavian productivity and Russian resistance to local conditions. But no. By profession he was an artificial inseminator. He delivered the full programme: selection techniques, efficiency management, factors affecting stillbirths. To townies like me talk about artificial insemination is slightly risqué. I can assure you that there are no sniggers to be had. I would never have believed semen was so boring. I yearned for the *frisson* of the reproductive mechanism of the potato.

Klang introduced me to Inge and Lolla, calves he had fathered, so to speak. They had other little brothers and sisters on the way. I have never been a sucker for sweet faces and big brown eyes with curly lashes after I was licked by a calf in my pushchair. Since then I have to look away from a cow's tongue on a butcher's counter and I still have nightmares about slobbery slugs crawling over my face. But I was intrigued. Were the marquetry cows family portraits? Did he have a favourite? Did he eat beef? But we had only just met. Instead, I asked what turned out to be the killer question. He could not evade the answer: the dark secret that haunted his daylight hours and kept him awake at night.

"What do you do with the milk?"

Had he been English or Russian he would have spun a tale, put on a gloss, evaded the question, prevaricated or lied. But he was a straight-talking Nordic. "We throw it away."

That was not entirely accurate. He fed some back to his own cows and to any local livestock farmer who had the transport to come and get it. But for most of the milk he had no pasteurizing mechanism, no packing facility, no transport, no means of getting the milk to a retail market. The dairy plant we could see from his yard could not use it, they said, because it was too rich and not approved for Russian consumption, since the cows were fed antibiotics not sanctioned for use in Russia. Klang said this was not true, that the milk was approved, but the managers stuck with their Russian suppliers because they got payoffs. When the ground thawed he could spray the milk on the fields, but in winter he kept it in polythene storage tanks, like big plastic bags, enormous udders of frozen milk. He was paid by European taxpayers to create a little European milk lake, a milk pond.

Far from showing Russians the future, this recalled the absurdities of Soviet Central Planning, when businesses had to meet production targets regardless of whether their stuff was wanted. I felt sorry for him, plonked down in the countryside like one of Natasha's aliens with only his pretty cows for company. I didn't know what to say. It was more to fill the awkward silence than with any serious intent that I blurted out: "Let's make it into mozzarella and sell it to Pizza Hut."

He wasn't meant to take it seriously. But straight talkers are straight listeners. They have no ear for the ironic, the playful, the insincere, the very stuff of an Englishman's discourse. Klang looked at me and nodded. "Hmm, *ja-juste*. It is a good idea."

A good idea. I was suckered. I have become inured to being told that my ideas are rubbish. On the rare occasion that somebody says "It's a good idea", especially a straight-talking Nordic, I feel the wonderful buzz that you get on the computer when Solitaire plays out and all the cards come waterfalling down and Congratulations flashes.

"I know someone at Pizza Hut. They've opened their second restaurant in Moscow. They have plans for three more. They are going into St Petersburg. What is their main ingredient apart from flour? Mozzarella cheese. Where do they get the cheese? Germany. Can you make mozzarella with your milk?"

"*Ja*, a good cheese maker can make any cheese you want. He can make it in your bath."

"Will your Union send us a cheese maker?"

"It is possible."

"We'll get Pizza Hut to pay for the equipment. We'll buy a van and deliver the cheese. We'll do the invoicing. We'll take care of everything. It's got to be cheaper than German cheese. And it's great publicity for Pizza Hut, encouraging local industry, blah blah blah."

"Who is *we*?

"TAMKO. Our company."

Over milk and Swedish meatballs, we sat at his kitchen table to draft proposals and wish away our lives in cheese-mongering. We were so caught up there was no time to see the Blok estate at Shakhmatovo. Klang drove me to the motorway junction where Natasha was waiting. I asked if she had been abducted by aliens and if they had given her lunch.

"Dzhorn! You believe in nothing. Only your stupid potatoes."

"That's not true. Right now I believe in cheese. I'll be the Czar of Cheese."

"I think you have no guardian angels."

"I'm sure I have one, like everybody else."

"Only one? I am sorry for you. I have thirty-three."

"Gosh."

"Some people have many more."

"Lucky them. How do they know?"

"By their star map when they were born."

"I thought one would be enough to keep you out of trouble."

"You cannot have too many. Especially in Moscow. You must be very careful."

My friend Gloria at Pizza Hut thought it was a good idea. She helped me draft a proposal to her regional head office in Poland. We asked for a one-year contract to supply mozzarella and whatever other cheese they required at local cheese prices plus the cost of transport. We also asked them to supply basic cheese-making equipment in return for massive endorsement from the Farmers' Union, the municipality of Solnechnogorsk, the mayor of Moscow and so on. Meanwhile, Klang confirmed that the Swedes would send over experts and set up a training programme for aspiring cheese makers. It wasn't going to make TAMKO rich, but it would give a boost to our Jackets project and surely line us up for consultancies with fat per diems.

The initial reaction from Warsaw was positive. Gloria told me to await a summons for a presentation and a meeting. There's nothing like a bit of success for putting a whistle in the lips and a spring in the stride. The Cheese Czar of Muscovy was not the culmination of a life's ambition, but it was a start. At such times the imagination lets rip. Jackets would have an Italian Mozzarella Special. We would design a label around Inge and Lolla. TAMKO would be Suppliers of Cheese to the Kremlin. I would be able to hold my head high in the Metropole Hotel. I went round car showrooms looking at refrigerated vans.

Gloria called me with the bad news. European central office had canned the idea. They would continue importing German mozzarella. The economics were ruthless. To reduce its cheese mountain the European Union dumped as much as it could in foreign markets. Not only did the Common Agricultural Policy keep German cheese farmers in business with subsidies, it subsidized the export of their overproduction. They paid Pizza Hut to take cheese into Russia. We could give our Russian cheese away for free and it would still not undercut the Germans. For cheese you can read butter and meat and all the other lakes and mountains the EU dumps on the rest of the word, destroying local markets, driving local farmers out of business, making it impossible for local producers and manufacturers to get going. And then they had the nerve to make measly development grants that pay consultants to live in the Metropole and lecture locals on entrepreneurship.

I delivered the bad news in person. I went on the train one Saturday and Klang picked me up from the station. I was introduced to his new offspring, Benbo, a sweet child but a male and destined for the abattoir as soon as he put on weight. Klang was resigned to our failure and refused to blame the European Union. Farmers don't bite the hand that subsidizes them. After milk and meatballs he drove me to Shakhmatovo. The estate was closed for renovation. I peered in the gates and through a gap in a fence at trees and frosted grass.

By the time I got back to Leningradsky station I had put things in perspective. Guardian angels work in mysterious ways. There is an awful moment when the Big One collapses into pieces, when feasibility turns into risibility. Only slightly less awful is when it takes off and you realize how much hard graft is involved in making it happen. Mozzarella didn't seem like such a Big Idea after all.

Do the fish go to Florida?

The first serious snowfall of winter came on the last Saturday night of October. On Sunday morning the apartment was brimming with light. I scuffed to the window in bare feet. The snow was falling, great floury flakes beating against the window, lured by the cotton-wool decoy on the sill between the double glazing.

A man wearing a white apron and chef's hat over an anorak and ski hat was selling something in the square below from a handcart. He had been there long enough for the snow to have covered the wheel tracks. There was no one else in sight. He waited stock still, turning into a snowman.

I put on my hat and coat over my pyjamas and went downstairs. It was bitterly cold. I plodded over to him wishing I had dressed properly. He stared at me with coal-black eyes. A dewdrop made the beginning of an icicle from the tip of his carrot-red nose.

"You look like a snowman," I said.

"A man has to live." He seemed to have no interest in selling me anything from under the white cloth that covered his wares. I had to lift it myself. Eggs.

"Are they fresh?"

"In this weather? They will last until spring."

"That's not what I asked. Are they fresh? Or are they second-grade fresh?"

"Laid this morning."

"Where?"

"Out of a chicken's arse."

"So they are fresh."

"Their little arses? I wipe them with cologne every morning."

I hadn't brought a bag with me so I picked out only four, two in each hand. We juggled them between us since neither of us had the common sense to put them down while I took out money and handed it over and he gave me change. When we finished he put the cloth back and stood stock-still again, letting the snow settle on his head and shoulders.

"Aren't you cold?"

"What do you think?"

Russian fortitude. Obstinacy. Determination. He would stand there until the eggs were gone or he disappeared in a drift until spring. Catherine the Great stationed a hundred Imperial Guards round the Winter Palace in the depths of winter. At night a score would die of cold at their posts. The next night they would be replaced and another score would freeze to death.

People took out winter clothes and aired out the camphor; greased boots and skates and skis; overhauled the snow shovel; laid in cans and jars from street markets; patched quilts; put fresh cotton wool on the ledge inside the double glazing to mop up condensation; took cars indoors and jacked them up to keep the tyres round. The metro was crowded with fair-weather drivers and weather-beaten *dachniks* hefting bags of home-grown produce, bedding, kitchen stuff.

My Russian friends did not share my loathing of snow. As I became sullen they became cheerful. While the cold brought on my rheumatism and depression, they believed it killed germs and made them strong. I wished I had learned to skate, I might not have fallen over so often. I never left home without Vibram soles, but they didn't do me much good. I staggered along from handhold to handhold while natives skipped past me on smooth plastic soles. Even the drunks were steadier than me. An old lady crossed me over the road, thinking I was blind. The worst places were outside stations, rinks of polished black slipperiness that you forgot about when you came up the escalator.

I tried to be positive. I learned to eat ice cream outside, sauntering along licking a cornet at 20 below. It was part of going native, like eating *kasha* without gagging.

At the office I commiserated with Afanasy about his hobby. "What do you do for fishing in the winter?"

"I fish."

"Where? Isn't everything frozen?"

"Jarn, do the fish go to Florida? Where do you think they are?"

★

"Under the ice?"

"By no means. Nice and cosy. That's where we get 'em. You never been ice fishin'? You wanna go?"

For sensible people the "try anything once" adage only goes so far. I knew before I tried it that ice fishing should be on my personal list of exclusions up there with nude paint-balling, bestiality with chickens and giving up wine. Why did I accept? I have no idea.

It was arranged for the following Saturday. Afanasy told me to wrap up warm and I took no chances: string vest, long-sleeved wool vest, T-shirt, wool shirt, sleeveless pullover, thick sweater, underpants, long johns, pyjamas, wool trousers, padded waterproofs, double ski gloves, long woolly scarf over my head under the astrakhan hat with earflaps down. And over the top of all of it my overcoat. Mallory went up Everest in less. I moved like a cosmonaut on a space walk.

I took the *elektrichka* from Savyolovsky station at eight o'clock and got off after a few stops in a suburb to the north of Moscow. As I wish never to go there again, I have expunged all record of the name. Afanasy met me at the station. It was not easy to manoeuvre my padded frame into his steamed-up Lada. I am not sure where he drove us, what with the state of the windows and the sweat pouring into my eyes. After twenty minutes or so he parked in a ploughed lay-by beside a wall of snow.

We got out. It was grey and misty. Afanasy said it wasn't cold, only about 15 below. Balmy to him, but to me it botoxed the face and knifed deep into the bronchioles and iced the perspiration under my swaddling.

Afanasy was no longer the dude from Brighton Beach. From his hat to his boots he was clad in sheepskin, fleece side in. He looked like a giant shammy.

I scrambled up the snow bank and he handed up our gear from the boot. An enormous corkscrew four foot long and a foot wide. A quiver of rods. A couple of pieces of wood nailed onto short bits of broomstick to sit on, like squat shooting sticks, that he called goat's legs. A home-made wooden box with a leather carrying strap.

We were beside a vast sheet of ice whose edges were lost all round in white mist. I don't know if it was a lake or a river and I couldn't ask because my teeth were gritted under my scarf to stop them chattering. I trod in his foot-steps across crunchy snow, deep and crisp and even, and onto the rink. Not falling over was the first challenge. I shuffled bow-legged, arms as outstretched as my clothing would allow. Around us were the huddled figures of other fishermen, scattered, one to a hole, anchorites in silent contemplation.

The bank was lost in the mist behind us when Afanasy called a halt. He looked round with a sigh of satisfaction and opened the box. He took out two bottles of vodka and handed one to me. We unscrewed and took a swig. As always *the first slug went down the gullet like a wooden stick,* but was infinitely preferable to freezing air. We took a second slug, the one that *goes down like a falcon,* and I felt better.

Afanasy got to work on the ice. Like the rest of his stuff the augur looked homemade, a twist of sharpened steel and an axe handle bolted horizontally across the top for turning. He laboured to little apparent effect when suddenly the blade bit and he was through. The ice was about a foot thick. Clear, greenish water lapped and gurgled. He gave me a rod out of the canvas bag, a metal stick with a reel soldered to the thick end. It was less than two feet long. There's not a lot of casting and trawling to be done in a hole a foot wide. On the business end of the line was a triple hook soldered to what looked like a handleless spoon. *Mormishka*, he said, which I took to be the name of the lure and not an endearment. My previous experience of fishing had been periods of intense boredom punctuated by impaling wriggly things on the hook, so a permanent metal fixture was a relief.

The next challenge was to perch on the goat's leg. Because of my padding I couldn't reach round to my backside, so Afanasy had to steer me onto it like a geriatric on a commode. It was extremely uncomfortable, not because of the seat, which I couldn't feel through the layers, but because of the need to keep my legs tense so I wouldn't fall off. Afanasy told me to lower the hook to the bottom, raise it three inches and keep it jiggling, like a shrimp. The rod should be constantly vibrating. The first part was difficult because I couldn't feel anything through my gloves. The second part was easy and he congratulated me on my technique. I didn't tell him it was because I was shivering.

He left me perched over my hole and bored his own a couple of yards away. Unable to move because of my clothes, lower body tensed on the goat leg, upper body jiggling the rod, I experienced myself solidifying. I couldn't feel my face. My limbs had that ominous sensation just before you get cramp in bed. The best I can think of to describe the rest of my body is necrosis. I began to under-stand the meaning of frost-hardened and why farmers looked the way they did.

One of the first rules of survival in extreme cold is never to drink alcohol. It opens the blood vessels and makes you colder faster. To hell with that. *The third slug went down like a little bird.* The saying is silent as to subsequent slugs, but each was more attractive than the last.

"Jarn, jiggle the rod."

I couldn't. I was so cold I had stopped shivering. Only the DTs would get me shaking again. Through frosted lashes I saw Afanasy yank fish after fish out of his hole, lovely silver things that flapped around on the ice in agony and died. I didn't care. To stave off the sweet drowsiness of hypothermia I concentrated on what Afanasy was telling me about fish – their names and habits and habitats and all the different ways of catching them under the ice in rivers and lakes and the sea. It was like pinching yourself to keep awake when you're driving, pain preferable to oblivion. All good things… and bad ones too.

Had I been able to through the icicles, I would have wept tears of relief when Afanasy stood up. He was very kind, extricating the rod from my hands and pulling me to my feet. I stood up like a cedilla. When we walked onto the ice I was a head taller than him. When we walked off I only came up to his shoulder.

He invited me home for hot soup and fried fish. We were only half an hour away. The heater on full blast just made me feel colder.

Afanasy's apartment complex had a row of wooden garages, the doors secured with arrays of locks and bars and chains. Before he drove the car in he invited me to look at his collection of fishing stuff at the back. There were rods and traps, feeders and nets, and smokers to deal with the catch. Like the augur and the rods, it was all home made. He took out of his pocket the *mormishka* he had just been using.

"See dis? My Dad made it. He fed the family with it. By no means. We woulda starved. He made everythin'."

"Did you live in the country?"

"Moscow. He lost a leg in the war. What job could he get? He taught me you want somethin', you make it. My wife and daughter I feed too. Fresh fish. Through the deficits it kept us goin'. By no means. She goes on at me to make more money but what good is money? Can you eat money?"

For once I was grateful that his apartment was overheated. I stripped down to three layers, checked in the mirror that I hadn't left my ears on the ice, and waited for my extremities to rejoin the rest of me. The narrow hall was crowded with fishy things and photographs. A six-foot varnished sturgeon hung from the ceiling.

Afanasy went into the bedroom to take off his sheep and I went into the living room. I was expecting more fish. Instead, my first thought was the Massacre of the Innocents. An otherwise unremarkable room was a charnel house of little heads and limbs and torsos in various stages of dismemberment. Tots and tinies in their best dresses lay where they fell on every flat surface. A table was heaped with little clothes and fabrics.

"My wife, Ludmilla."

"Is she a puppeteer?"

"She makes dolls."

"Quite a hobby."

"By no means. She makes a fortune."

I followed him into the kitchen. He clattered around and microwaved a meaty soup to keep us going while he gutted the morning's catch.

"Where does Ludmilla sell her dolls?"

"Houston. Phoenix. San Diego. They love 'em over there. Antique dolls is big business. Big collectors. They pay a lot of money. By no means. They love old Russian dolls."

Over soup and beer and fried fish with gherkins, he told me about Ludmilla's business. In the early days of street trading, antiques of all kinds could be picked up for nothing. Ludmilla had a doll that had belonged to her great-grandmother. In the Izmailovsky Park flea market a Texan woman called Marcia gave her ten dollars for it. Ludmilla couldn't believe her luck. The American walked away and came back. She said she couldn't give her ten dollars, it wouldn't be right. Ludmilla was ready to fight to keep the bill, make a scene, call the police. The American said she would give her another ten if she came to her hotel. In her room Marcia showed her the other old dolls she had bought. Back in Houston they were worth up to a thousand dollars.

Ludmilla went into business with her. She scoured the markets for antique dolls. She made trips to other cities, built up a network of suppliers, became an expert in restoring them. She found craftsmen who could work in china and wax and wood. As the supply of genuine articles dried up, the craftsmen made replicas out of old materials. She found old fabrics and threads and learned how to make the clothes in authentic ways. She taught other miniature dress makers. A year ago she went to a convention in Houston and made direct contact with collectors, by-passing Marcia.

"Amazing. What an entrepreneur. What a case study. I'd love to meet her. When will she be back?"

"Coupla months, probly. They got conventions this time a year. She's getting our daughter into college."

"How long has she been away?"

"I toldya. About a year ago. By no means."

Afanasy huddled over his fishing rod summer and winter, feeding a family who would never come back. I didn't know what to say.

"Would you ever go out and join them?"

"They'll come back. *Dry bread at home is better than roast meat abroad.*"

"So are these fish. They're very tasty, Afanasy."

187

The goats are guarding the cabbage

We identified several private farms that could grow potatoes for us from the seeds we gave them. Financing was a serious problem. They could get grants for plant and equipment from the Union, but they still had to find financing for running costs, fertilizer and so on. In the West they would get seasonal credit from banks. Our suppliers had no experience and no established market for their produce. While they had a right to their land in a sort of lease, they could not mortgage it, as all land remained the property of the state. No bank manager worth his two-hour lunch would lend to such a prospect. So when the chance came to find financing for the farms, I took it.

I was looking forward to a quiet afternoon, catching up on paperwork, drinking tea, eating cabbage *pirozhki*, practising my Russian, watching television with the secretaries, staring out of the window at the falling snow, reading Chekhov, doing the puzzles in the *Moscow Times*. I was on my second glass of tea when Natasha summoned me to the professor's office. His secretary, a well-endowed girl with big hair, was doing something intricate with her fingernails, so didn't give me a glance when I knocked on the professor's door and walked in. He was shaking hands with three enormous men.

"Why, come and see us. Before the football season's over."

"Hmmm. Do you have ice hockey?"

"We got the St Louis Blues."

They turned and looked at me like defensive tackles eyeing a rookie quarterback. A combined 750-pound dressed weight of superior corn-fed well-hung well-marbled certified prime Midwestern cowman, bursting with vitamins, probiotics and growth hormones. Mail-order grey suits with tube jackets and turn-ups above the ankles. Matching tie and top-pocket handkerchief. Short-sleeved white button-down shirt with a red pack of Marlboro in the pocket. They were an awesome sight. The professor didn't introduce us and they plodded out in single file.

"Hmmm, Mister John, you were a banker. Please, we would like your proposals for a Farmers' Bank. There are 60,000 private farms in Russia and the banks will not lend to them. We have to make our own bank."

"Why don't you find a European bank to advise you? The French are good at that sort of thing."

"We have a proposal from Land O'Lakes. Those were the men. They will set a bank up for us with branches in each *oblast*."

"Then why ask me?"

"Hmm, we want a second opinion."

★

Land O'Lakes, based in St Louis, Missouri, is the biggest cooperative in the world. Its logo is an Indian maiden recursively offering a pack of butter with the logo of an Indian maiden offering a pack of butter with the logo of an Indian maiden… It dominates the dairy business. I sniffed per diems over the horizon. Perhaps I could get involved with the project. It was ten years since I had escaped banking and in any case I knew nothing about agricultural lending. I reckoned two weeks would be long enough to bone up.

"Of course. When shall I come back?"

"Twelve o'clock."

"What?"

"We have a meeting of a deputation of the Council of Economic Regeneration. We have the deputy mayors of ten Russian cities. It will be a good opportunity to discuss the proposals."

I had exactly an hour to develop a presentation or a sudden illness. Less the twenty minutes when my mind went a complete blank. *He who takes no risks never gets to drink champagne.* I decided to go back to the fundamentals of banking, ask the audience how they applied to farmers, and hope that I could swing it out until they went for lunch.

We gathered in the main conference room. I was to speak in English with Natasha for consecutive translation. Twenty men sat in rows with politely glum expressions, hands folded across their stomachs, a posse of deputies – Deputy Mayors, Deputy Minister of Agriculture, Deputy Chairman of Moscow District Agricultural Council,

Deputy Governors, four plain and simple Deputies from the Parliament. I have ransacked my files and my diary for the name of the Deputy Mayor of St Petersburg. Two men had just been appointed to that office. One was Vladimir Putin, but I don't think he was there as I would have remembered him, since he resembles my fellow Brummie and Blues supporter, the comedian Jasper Carrott.

I stood at a flip chart, jacket off, mind blank, sniffing the felt-tip for courage. First, the professor explained the problem. In theory, Russian banks were supposed to lend to private farms at 20 per cent. But they could earn 300 per cent on lending overnight to other banks. Their excuse was that farmers were not creditworthy. What could be done? The professor sat down. Over to me. I took a deep breath, mastered the liquefaction of my innards, ignored the pounding heart and perspiring brow and started.

"Well, er, um, what is a bank?"

Thank God for consecutive translation – precious moments to think of what to say next. I started off with the fundamental job of banks: to look after other people's money. This was startling news to my audience. Brought up under the old system of centralized planning, they thought that banks were mechanisms for dishing out the state's largesse.

I have to say this was one of the few occasions when I have impressed myself. I have often winged it but rarely taken flight. I started out at the flip chart in a state of near total ignorance and when I finished I had learned as much as anyone.

The gist of my story was that the Union did not need a bank. Who would run it? They would need premises and safes and guards and clerks and credit analysts and systems. They would have to survive in the chaotic Russian money markets. What the Union needed was a Guarantee Corporation, which would guarantee loans to farmers. The Union would pool the collective risk of their members. If they could wheedle a government guarantee so much the better – banks would have no excuse not to lend, in fact they could classify the loans as government securities that they had to hold by law. The Union would do what it was good at, evaluating the viability of its members.

I finished, my shirt damp, heady with adrenaline and high on felt-tip fumes. I slumped in a chair. The others were huddled in a circle talking too fast and too low for me to understand. Finally, the professor stood up.

"We like your ideas. Please, we would like you to put it into practice."

"What about Land O'Lakes?"

"Your idea is better. I will tell them tomorrow."

The satisfaction of putting one over on the Yanks was overshadowed by the enormity of what I had taken on. The Russian financial market was a mystery. I reassured myself that I was little different from other advisers parachuted in from the West to put the Russians right. But unlike them, I wasn't being paid. Either I had to palm the project off onto someone else or find a gravy train to hop onto.

The first step was to establish credibility. I persuaded the professor to hire me as a employee of the Union, a *rabotnik*. The contract was approved by the central committee of the Trade Union of Agricultural Workers and regulated by Russian labour laws. I was entitled to Russian holidays, free Russian medical care, and a week in a sanatorium if I stayed more than three years. If this wasn't incentive enough, I had a salary of 10,000 roubles a month. This was more than twice the national average, three times the pay of a university lecturer and twice that of a middle-ranking civil servant. When I signed the contract 10,000 roubles was worth $50. After three months it was worth $25.

With a Union business card and an outline for a feasibility study, I called at the office of the Representative of the European Union. A helpful young man explained that the Representative had his own budget for smaller projects that he could approve locally. He told me what to say in the application and was optimistic that we would be successful. I delivered the form that afternoon. Buoyed with hope, I got down to some basic research.

I wanted to talk to a bank outside Moscow that had farmers as customers, so Afanasy fixed me up with the newly established Komprombank in Orekhovo-Zuyevo, fifty miles east of Moscow. "Newly established bank" was as much of a cliché as "onion-domed church" or "frozen steppe". In 1988 there were five banks in Russia. Five years later there were over two thousand.

Orekhovo-Zuyevo had been a textile town since the eighteenth century. Under the Morozovs, Old Believers and

new industrialists, it boomed in the second half of the
nineteenth century. Now on harder times, there were still
old mills and mansions and handsome workers' housing
among crumbling Soviet monoliths. The headquarters and
only branch of Komprombank was the pre-revolutionary
Merchants' Club. The Communist Party used it as a guest
house. Two years ago they sold it to a consortium of privatized state businesses for their new bank.

It was a lumpish red-brick building making three sides
of a courtyard. A neoclassical portico was stuck on the
front, topped by a weatherworn goddess with a torch illu-
minating the triumph of Commerce, Communism or
Capitalism, depending on the era. Milling in the courtyard
was the usual mob that hung around public buildings:
drivers, messengers, beggars, drunks, old women selling
pies and cigarettes in singles, and a score of people with
legitimate business, pleading to be let in by bouncers in
long leather coats. Natasha and I were on the guest list. In a
marbled hall, toughs in sharp grey suits took our coats and
ushered us into the antechamber of the general manager,
where two decorative secretaries attended to his needs,
their manicures and the daytime soaps. All trace of the
building's Communist past had been washed out in pale
pink and cream.

Sergei Artemovich came out to greet us. Little and
round and jowly and bald, he affected half-moon spectacles, a heavy three-piece suit and a watch chain. He looked
like a relic of the Merchants' Club, straight out of a
Capitalist Enemy of the People poster of the 1920s. He ush-

ered us into his sanctum and we sat down in front of his desk on upholstered mahogany. The walls were covered with the dark panelling with which bankers the world over hope to convince us they are trustworthy. The desk had two telephones, black and green. He ignored the black when it rang, bongoeing his fat fingers on the arm of his chair until one of the secretaries risked their nails to pick it up. When the green rang he plucked it up and stood to attention and spoke in hushed, urgent tones. This was the power of the telephone seen at the receiving end.

"Oh, Mister John Mole, you are English? You know the Chyarnocks?"

"Um…"

"Of Blackburn Lancashire. Very famous in Orekhovo-Zuyevo. They made the Blue and Whites. You must know them. They brought grass from England. It is a pleasure to meet their countryman."

I had no idea what he was talking about but rode the goodwill. I discovered later that, like many industrialists at the time, the Morosovs hired British managers. Harry Charnock from Blackburn came over with his nephews. Keen on soccer, they founded the first Russian football club in 1894. They built the ground and imported turf from England. The Orekhovo club still plays on it. They were founder members of the first Russian league, the Moscow League, which they won several times before the Revolution. Bruce Lockhart, diplomat, secret agent and writer, played for them and won a championship medal in 1912. The future Field Marshal Earl Wavell also turned out for the team. They still play in blue and white, the colours of Blackburn Rovers.

Calling on banks had been my bread and butter for years, so I felt at home. Over fine china cups we inquired about the health of the rouble and the dollar, the prospect for interest rates and the whereabouts of gold and oil prices, like two old aunties discussing their relatives. Sergei Artemovich did everything possible not to lend to farms. The payment system was so bad that it took up three months to get a loan into the borrower's account. It took two weeks to transfer money among branches of the same bank.

The financial system was choking business. It tied up working capital, pushed up the demand for credit, dried up cash flow and made self-financing impossible. Because of rampant inflation, money halved its value every three months. Businesses immediately spent their cash on goods, so they were usually illiquid. All this was strangling private enterprise at birth, as I reported in an article called "Enemies of Enterprise" for a British newspaper. I showed it to Oleg and suggested he put it into *Izvestia* and the *Moscow Business Times* to puff the credentials of ICBM.

"*Znachet*, this is very good for foreigners to read. But it is horseradish. It will make Russians laugh. *The goats guard the cabbage*. These banks are set up as money pots for their owners. They dip their hands in like kiddies in a sweetie jar. Borrowing money at a good rate is easy. If bank manager gives you money you give him a nice bribe. If he does not give you money you kill him."

Banking is a high-risk business. In the past ten years more than 300 bankers have been murdered. I have often wondered if Sergei Artemovich is still with us.

I called the EU office about the funding application. It had been approved in principle. All it needed was the Representative's signature, but he had been called back urgently to Brussels before he could get his pen out. He never returned. There was loose talk, gossip, rumour: shady deals, a Russian mistress, dummy companies, slush funds, dodgy deals, sweeteners. Accusations were retracted before they had been made. Things were swept under carpets. Skeletons were bundled into cupboards. Nothing was found, nothing was alleged. It was all based on malice and misunderstanding. But auditors swarmed over the office and local grants were suspended indefinitely.

I was indignant. I was self-righteous. I was secretly pleased. What seemed a great idea on a flip chart would have been a nightmare in practice. *It looked smooth on paper, but we forgot the ravines.* The main problem was not the creditworthiness of the farms but the banking system. My proposal was a bad idea. Of course I didn't say this in my report to the professor. I weaselled on about money supply, reserve ratios and so on, with sideswipes at the EU for not financing further research. My recommendation was that the Farmers' Union should consider setting up its own network of banks. I suggested that it ask for assistance from another institution with experience of agricultural lending. A Western cooperative perhaps? It was just an idea.

My employment contact was never formally terminated. Technically I am still a *rabotnik*. I have four weeks in a sanatorium owing to me.

Am I coconut?

Getting information about market trends, commodity prices, supplies and farming capabilities was not easy. In countries with a tradition of secrecy, official statistics are eager to please but not to inform. Hard information is a commodity to be traded. Free information is not to be trusted. You don't give away the good stuff unless there is something in return. And you certainly don't gab to strangers.

Mustard Flor did his best to help me. Over the bitter coffee he brewed behind his shelves of unreliable statistical journals I enjoyed his conversation, a disarming combination of intelligence and naïvety. He asked me about this Western company or that international organization and whether they were hiring economists. I gave him such plausible advice that he treated me like a wise uncle on many other serious matters.

"Ah, Mister John, why does dollar bill have pyramid and eye? Are all Americans Freemasons?"

"Ah, Mister John, is it true that Jimi Hendrix was Cherokee Indian?"

"Ah, Mister John, you know America, what is difference between horseshit, bullshit, ratshit and chickenshit?"

One day he came into my office on the fifth floor. Struggling with conflicting data on potato prices in the Black Lands, the fertile crescent of Southern Russia, I was glad of the interruption. He asked what I was doing on the following Saturday. A wise person answers such a question by stalling and fudging until they find out what is being proposed. But I wasn't thinking and he was delighted that I had no plans.

"Please be my guest at Tchaikovsky Symphonic Theatre."

I passed the theatre on my way to work. It was a grey-stone barracks of a building on the corner of Tverskaya and the Inner Ring. Except for his ballet music I like Tchaikovsky, although I hoped they were not doing the *1812*.

"I'd love to. What are they playing?"

"It is State Troupe of the Autonomous Republic of Udmurtia."

"Oh. Ah. How nice."

I kicked myself for not stalling and fudging. It was too late now. One of my earliest black-and-white television memories is the Red Army Choir at the London Palladium, Cossacks squatting and kicking their legs out and beefy chaps in AA patrolman uniform belting out the "Volga Boat Song". I was not impressed then and nothing I have seen since has converted me to manufactured folklore, from *Riverdance* to Chinese opera.

The name Udmurtia sounded so improbable outside a Tintin story that for a moment I hoped it was a satire based on dire Soviet national culture shows. But Udmurtia is all too real, an autonomous republic in the middle of the Urals, famous for steel and locomotives and Kalashnikov rifles. It has its own language, Udmurt, in the same family as Finnish and Hungarian. Flor was born in the capital, Izhevsk. His father was a Muscovite and his mother Udmurt. They moved to Moscow when Flor was ten and shortly afterwards his father left them. His mother did not want to give up their precious Moscow *propiska* and the chance for Flor to go to Moscow State University, so they remained exiles. His mother had died a few months before, so saloon-bar psychology suggested that the show was part of the mourning process.

"Ah, Mister John, you will like it very much," he threatened. "Udmurt culture is wonderful. We have music and singing and dancing."

And colourful frocks and funny hats and hand clapping and plinky-plonk music on peculiar instruments and inventive ways of doing the splits. Ah well. There would be *shampanskoe* and red caviar canapés at the interval. Look on the bright side.

"And you will meet my girlfriend, Maria. She speaks very good English. She wants to go to America."

It would be just the three of us, an odd combination. I could see why he would show off his cultural heritage to his girlfriend and to a curious foreigner, but not to both at the same time.

We arranged to meet at Belaruskaya metro station, green line, direction Krasnogvardeyskaya, last carriage. I was there first and when they appeared I thought her appearance was a trick of the artificial light. She was the first Goth I had seen in Moscow. Pancake-white face, purple lipstick, red-rimmed eyes, rats' tails of long black hair shot with silver braid, long black dress, black shawl. A green woolly hat and a standard-issue maroon Russian overcoat marred the vampirish effect, but it was 20 below outside. Under it all she was very attractive with high cheekbones and very blue eyes.

"Hi, I'm happy to meet you, I'm Maria, how are you today?"

"*Orchen priadna.* How do you do?"

"I'm good? I hope we didn't keep you waiting too long?" She spoke like Voice of America, enunciating statements as questions, but with the stern expression that Russians put on when they first meet.

"Mister John was many years in America," said Flor, and I understood why I had been invited. She was crazy about the US. If I had known I would have come in a parka and baseball cap. I didn't even have any gum to chew. I hoped she would not be disappointed.

"Oh wow? Where?"

"Nooyawk. Ellay," I drawled.

"Oh wow?"

Actually I'd spent most of my time in Pittsburgh, the Izhevsk of the Midwest, but I was trying to help Flor out. Nervous at first, he relaxed on the way to the theatre as Maria and I discussed our preferences for bagels over muffins, the ocean over the coast, Morrison over Jagger.

"Me, I'm heavy metal?" she said.

"I saw Aerosmith once."

"Wow, I don't believe it? In Central Park?"

"Pittsburgh Civic Arena."

We had good seats in the front of the first balcony. The inside of the theatre was as grey and functional as the outside. The audience were ordinary Moscow folk out for an evening's entertainment. The same audiences with the same taste in music, hairstyles and clothes were at *The Sound of Music* in Watford Civic Centre, *Jesus Christ Superstar* at the Dortmund Staatsoper, *Oklahoma!* at Heinz Hall in Pittsburgh. Maria the Goth could not have stood out more in ballgown and tiara.

The State Troupe of Udmurtia lived up to every misgiving. The national costume was a confection of Turkic flounce and Celtic Tartan. Their music sounded like national music everywhere, cover versions of the same dozen old European tunes and jigging rhythms. We had the Udmurt versions of the maypole and the floral dance and the eightsome reel with hand slapping and foot stamping. In between the dance numbers a young woman with a flowing headdress and a zither on her knee sang about wild swans. A white-haired bard declaimed some complicated business involving a green man of the forest taking a human bride away on the back of a bear with a bull riding on a fish. A lad with a balalaika charmed a crescent moon out of the sky for his lover, or perhaps it was his dead lover, I didn't quite catch the drift. It was the usual stuff you find from the Atlantic to the Urals, the Baltic to the Med.

I tapped my feet and played arpeggios on my knees to show willing. Maria made no pretence. She looked like a vampire selecting her next victim among innocent villagers at play. Flor loved every cadence, every swirl, every hop and leap. The climax of the first half was a full-company rendition of *Udmurtia Miyam*, the national anthem, which had him applauding with tears in his eyes and shouting bravo.

The interval was difficult. I could sense a headache coming on, not in me but Maria. I felt it my duty to distract her until it was too late to say she was going home. While Flor queued for the demi-sec and canapés, I tried to find out what she saw in him.

"Where did you meet Flor?"

"We were classmates in high school? We live in the same apartment building? We did figure-skating lessons together?"

"Do you live with your family?"

"My mom?"

"What does she think of America?"

"All Russians wanna go to America? The difference is between those who make it happen and those who make wishes on the birthday cake?"

Flor came back with the refreshments looking excited. "Hey, there's big party afterwards. I meet my friend Alexei from Izhevsk. We go in his car. Some actors from the show will go. It will be big Udmurt party. We will have a good fun."

This was the moment for Maria's migraine/flu/fainting fit/fever to strike. I would insist on taking her home and

★

leave Flor to enjoy the show and the Udmurt reunion. But she didn't fall ill and condemned us both to the second half. She lapsed into more murderous brooding, I turned on false gaiety, Flor was transported. After a touching scene from an Udmurt epic in which the heroes get killed and come back to their girlfriends as big eagles and do the hokey-cokey, he turned to me with misty eyes and said that his mother would have loved it. I was happy for him, but very sad that he missed his mother and a little sad that he liked this stuff.

I queued up for the coats while Flor and Maria looked for Alexei. He was a fresh-faced lad with the broad shoulders and barrel chest of a wrestler. He led us to his car, a Peugeot 504 estate with three rows of seats. Nine of us got in. Maria had to press up close to me, which was pleasant. Our Udmurt friends, led by Flor, broke into song. It was a lot more raucous than what we had just been listening to and all the better for it.

We ground through a blizzard, Alexei crouched over the wheel, our breath misting up the windows, not that it made much difference with the state of his wipers and the horizontal snow. The journey was interminable and would have been insufferable if Maria had not found her most comfortable position with her thigh on mine and her head on my chest. In the stench of hot bodies and damp clothes, she smelled of warm raspberries. By the time we arrived my right side was asleep, my back was in spasm and I was in love.

W e piled out of the car into a factory courtyard. It was
littered with rusting machinery and looked disused,
but in Russia it is hard to tell. The concept of depreciation
is unknown, so assets are used until they fall apart. These
business-like thoughts were far from my mind as I slithered, bent and stiff, through the snow in pursuit of Maria,
like Quasimodo after Esmeralda.

We took a freight elevator up to the top floor and
stepped out into a Greenwich Village loft circa 1965: cranes
and tackles and bare light bulbs hanging from the ceiling, a
double bed on a platform made of packing cases, clothes
hanging on lines strung wall to wall, a drum kit, an industrial heater like a jet engine, tables made of trestles and
boards. In the middle of the floor was a wrestling mat. The
walls were sprayed in rainbow colours. It smelled of liniment and marijuana, beer and ripe trainers. Alexei's father
was the factory manager. When the money went out of
Russian sport and public facilities were privatized, he gave
the top floor to Alexei and his friends to practise in.

More people arrived, including some of the cast of the
show. We applauded them out of the elevator. They had
changed out of national into international costume, jeans
and leather jackets and trainers. Someone put on Led
Zeppelin. Alexei produced cases of beer, paper cups, loaves
of bread, onions and a massive salami. Vodka and cognac
were spirited out of coat pockets. The sweet smell of hash
mingled with Russian Marlboro. A quartet of Goths arrived,
but not even they could cheer up Maria who sat disconso-
late on the bed chain smoking. I sat down next to her.

"Cheer up."

"Is this like America?" she asked.

"Not any more. Rich people live in lofts now. Bankers. Media people. The sort who can't tell the difference between a life and a lifestyle."

"Russians have no lifestyle and no life? What can we do?"

"What Americans do. Get an analyst and a decorator."

Flor dragged me up to introduce me to his friends. I drifted round in his wake, remembering to look po-faced and not grinning like a half-wit. I washed up next to a pale, cadaverous man in black suit and shirt, immense purple bags under his eyes, lurking in the corner shadows. He offered me a joint. It was like an anti-drugs commercial. Say No to Death. As Rizlas were in short supply, stoners used Russian cigarettes, called *papirosa*, that have a hollow cardboard tube instead of a filter. A couple of flicks got rid of the tobacco and you refilled it with stuff. I declined. I have never mastered the technique of speaking while I held my breath. It was too much like the conversations on a chest ward.

"Good shit. Kazakh," he croaked in American English. "Grows wild on the steppe. Organic. Good for you."

"They use this in Udmurtia?"

"Use it all over. Kazakhs and Kirgiz and Uzbeks have smoked it for ever. Not even those Communist sonsabitches could stamp it out. You know how the Russians conquered them? They were smashed on vodka. Alcohol makes you aggressive. Grass makes you pacifist. Booze against grass."

"Are you from Izhevsk?"

"Chicago. My grandparents were from there. Sent out to learn the steel business in 1922 and stayed. I came back to help out the old country."

"What are you doing here?"

"Pizza Hut. You?"

"Jackets. Baked potatoes."

"Oh."

"It's a struggle to find raw materials here."

"Do what we do. We import everything from sauce to napkins."

"Let's have lunch."

"Sure."

The noise got too loud to talk. One of Alexei's wrestler friends started hammering the drums, as if the music wasn't loud enough already. I was out of my depth. I hadn't been to a party like this for twenty years and I didn't like them then. Maria had disappeared. I lurked in a corner on a packing case and wished I knew how to get home.

I escaped from the noise and fug down a corridor to a similar-sized loft, still used for storage by the factory. It served as the chill-out room in more senses than one, as it was unheated and must have been 20 below. It was like coming out of the sauna and diving into the cold pool. Flor was there, standing by himself at the window. I stood beside him and we watched the snow falling on factory roofs. Through the static was the Moscow River, frozen and snow covered, a swathe of nothingness through the city.

"Are you OK, Flor?"

"What are we doing, Mister John?"

"Having a good time?"

"Maybe," he sighed. I braced myself for an outpouring of Russian soul. "How would I do in America?"

"You'd do just fine." We stood and watched the snow while our body temperatures plummeted.

"Am I coconut, Mister John?"

"Er…"

"Coconut. Coconuts fall in sea and they go a thousand miles to another place and they grow there."

"One thousand five hundred people a year are killed by coconuts falling on their heads."

"Dear God."

"What is a coconut in Udmurt?"

"*Kokoos.*"

We went back to the party and I never saw Maria again. On Monday I left on a tour of the farms of the Leningrad district. I was away for three weeks.

The day I got back to the office I went down to see Flor. He was happy because a friend in the Izvestia News Agency had sent him a UN report on wheat production in the Former Soviet Union. I complimented him on a new silver tie, which shone like a fog light in his general mustardness.

"Thank you. My girlfriend gave it."

"How is Maria?"

"Not Maria. Katerina. Mister John, what are your plans for Saturday?"

"Saturday? Oh, I think a friend is getting tickets for the Bolshoi."

"Oh, that is pity."

"So who is Katerina? Is she Udmurt?"

"No, she is from Bashkortostan."

"Where?"

"Bashkortostan. Bashkiria. It is in Urals. Next to Udmurtia. She is like me, her father was Russian and her mother Bashkir, from Ufa." I knew about Bashkiria. Rudolf Nureyev was a Bashkiri Tatar.

"I see. Is the State Troupe of the Bashkortostan Republic in town?"

"No. Why do you say that? She is accordionist. On Saturday there is national accordion competition in Kremlin Theatre. It is pity you cannot come."

"What a shame. I love the accordion. Perhaps the next time. Tell me, what happened with Maria?"

"She is living with a Siberian in her grandmother's *dacha*."

"What? In this weather?"

"They have stove. Siberians have interesting mushrooms."

"But still."

"He says he is shaman. She wants to be a true Russian."

"I thought she wanted to be American."

"She said she could never be a true American. She was Russian pretending to be American."

"I hope it wasn't my fault."

"It was mine. I took her to Udmurt show. She said she was so moved she could not speak. She envied me to have

210

such heritage. She said it was such beautiful culture. She decided to discover her rootings. She wants to find Russian self."

"I'm sorry."

"It's OK. She gave me all her heavy metal. She said I should learn them if I want to go to America. But Katerina and I prefer accordion. Tell me, Mister John, do they play accordion in America?"

Free jazz

I should not like to give the impression that I was swanning around on taxpayers' money. There was serious work to be done, of a kind that brings a glaze to the eyes of the general reader, but I was assiduous. Fax machines in Moscow and Clapham chattered about yields and options, machinery specs, square footage and rentals, hourly wage rates and annual bonuses. I pored over weekly bulletins on produce prices from the Interfax news agency, market research reports, property newsletters, accounting regulations. We crafted cash flows and business plans, projections and simulations, forecasts and sensitivity analyses. We agonized over turnover per table, meals per occupancy, revenue per portion. I lay awake at night concocting menus, tossed and turned between the merits of cook-chill and frozen. I toyed with Desiree and Charlotte and Marfona into the small hours.

When I was preparing to write this book I dug my old files out of the shed. Hard information would give substance and a sense of mission to the story, I thought. The jewel was the report I submitted to the Know-How Fund, a thesis on fast-food franchising in the new Russia, a brilliant case study of the economics, politics and semiotics of the business and its

★

social context. A year's work. As I opened the file, disbelief gave way to to panic, which ceded to despair. My fax and computer used thermal printers. The immortal words had faded to white on the heat-sensitive paper. Every page I had saved was blank. It was a wonderful image of the futility of human endeavour. But bloody annoying.

Staffing was critical. Everyone in the business was unanimous that we should not hire anybody who had worked in a traditional Russian restaurant or shop. Service, with or without a smile, was an unknown concept to them. Employees helped themselves before the customer. Takings were reckoned up on the basis of one for them, one for me. Jobs were for life, so there was no disincentive to idleness and poor time-keeping. The only way to circumvent this culture was to hire nobody over 20 years old. Petya found us a core team of five friends from his college. We arranged to send them to London in the summer to work in Jackets.

Afanasy had a fishing friend who was a tax inspector. He briefed me on payroll management. The maximum amount of wages employers could set off against tax was $350 per employee per year. This was far below the going rate of $1200 for crew and $7500 for a manager. This meant that if all our wages went through the books we would end up paying the equivalent of 90 per cent tax on profits. In addition, employers paid 40 per cent of wages in tax and pensions and employees paid 12 per cent income tax. The result was that wages were paid in cash under the counter. There were many other ploys that depended on the compliance of the tax inspector. My favourite was that if you employed disabled people you didn't have to prepay your tax. What would disabled people do in a restaurant? Nothing. They would not exist. Like Gogol's dead souls, they would only be names on the staff roster. I looked forward to making them up.

We did market research. Flor's Bashkiri girlfriend dumped him. To cheer him up I took him with me and Natasha on fact-finding expeditions to our competition. I learned that a Russian restaurant was really a night club, a café was a restaurant, a *bufyet* was a snack bar, and the equivalent to a pub was a shack where they brewed their own beer in buckets. A rock-hard dried fish that you whacked on the edge of the table filled the culinary niche of a packet of peanuts. I paid Petya to recruit researchers and carry out a traditional market research study among young people. He came back with 100 per cent positive approval. He probably sat down and ticked all the boxes himself. I probed gently, but didn't make a big thing of it. He grew up in a system in which nobody cared about their opinions and attitudes. The whole idea of marketing, finding out what people want and making it for them, was as alien as it was in 1950s Britain.

To survey the expats, I went to the Thursday Night British Club at the back of the commercial section of the Embassy. It was a large room with about 100 seats around tables, two dartboards and a bar serving seven kinds of beer and three flavours of crisps. It was a home from home, if you patronized working men's clubs. It was not for EU consultants and government advisers, oil men and bankers, City lawyers and accountants, anyone on fat expenses. They hung round with the mafia and the *valutnaya* in the lobbies and bars of the Metropole and the Radisson.

The club was for honest toilers, whose per diems just covered their expenses, getting out of cheap hotels and seedy apartments for a couple of cans of McEwan's and a game of darts – like Keef, the Rolls-Royce engineer working at an airbase outside town, and Camilla, a young woman just graduated from my old college, who worked for IBM, and Wayne, who had just arrived from Tooting with a truckload of building materials parked outside. Old hands terrified the new arrivals with urban myths, such as people found naked and dead on garbage dumps after taking a cab from the airport, foreigners' apartment doors stove in by armed robbers with sledgehammers, friends of friends who had been gassed unconscious and robbed on overnight trains. But mostly you could pick up useful tips about making the most of this alien, confusing and exciting city. Those at the club would all have murdered a Jackets with extra cheese.

On my first evening I sat down next to a chap a bit older and a lot fitter than me, bald on top and grey round the edges, wearing a London Marathon T-shirt and a shiny red track suit. His Brummie twang made me feel homesick.

"Just arrived?"

"Off to Kyrgyzstan in the morning."

"Oh great. Do you live there?"

"No. Sutton Coldfield."

⭐

"Land of my fathers."

"What? Kyrgyzstan?"

"Birmingham."

"I'm setting up chambers of commerce."

Kyrgyzstan. A mountainous semi-desert country in Central Asia next to China. Cotton fields and Turkic tribes. Horseback rugby with a headless goat for a ball. Chambers of commerce were just what they needed.

"How are you getting on there?"

"It's my first time. I'll be there nearly a fortnight."

"So long? Do you speak Kyrgyz? Russian?"

"I speak a bit of French."

"That'll come in handy. I thought for a minute you were involved with sport. Don't know what gave me that idea."

"I was in the marathon. I went straight to the airport."

I was impressed. I loathe running. And I was envious. What a great caper. Central Asia. With fees and expenses and per diems dripping from the gravy train.

"My luggage got lost. This is all I've got. I'll look a real berk."

He needn't have worried. The shell suit is Kyrgyz national dress. I phoned him when I got back to England. He had launched a campaign to twin Sutton Coldfield with Kyrgyzstan's second city of Osh, on the basis that they are both noted for their television transmitters.

I went out into the street with a picture of the product and a clipboard. Russian reactions were mixed. Many of those who could afford to eat out preferred the chic of

McDonald's. Those who couldn't afford it would rather spend their money at the markets. One woman didn't believe the picture was a potato. A middle-aged man shouted at me for torturing honest Russians with fantasies. An old lady gazed at the photo, clutched her stomach and burst into tears. Ashamed, I gave her fifty roubles.

I stood outside the McDonald's in Pushkin Square with my clipboard sampling the queue that snaked around the building. There were about 700 seats inside and about half that number of people waiting to get in. By timing how long they waited, I calculated that the outlet served something like 30,000 meals on an average day. There was a lot less takeaway than in the West, perhaps 10 per cent of the trade. The food was too expensive for street grazing. A Big Mac Meal cost a tenth of the notional monthly wage. There was not much of a peak at mealtimes. Russians did not keep a rigorous timetable for food. If they were hungry or a meal came along, they ate it regardless of the time.

A quarter of the customers were foreigners, mainly tourists but a good sprinkling of expats. The Russians were predominantly under 50, well dressed, middle class, working in the private sector. There were still tour buses from hundreds of miles away come to taste the West, although they were less frequent than in 1990 when the place opened. I noted a coach from Volgograd, 600 miles away. Not long ago they would have been coming for Lenin's tomb. But I couldn't be snooty about them. In 1974 McDonald's opened its first British restaurant in Woolwich, along the South Circular from where we lived. We got the children into clean T-shirts and joined the queues. String fries not chip-shop chips, meat with cheese on it, toasted buns, eating out of cardboard – it was new and exciting and American. That was before trans fats and obesity and rainforests were thought about.

The queue in Pushkin Square was entertained by buskers. The best was a three-piece jazz band: trumpet, snare drum and banjo. They played mainly New Orleans, with "Midnight in Moscow" every fifth number. When he got bored the trumpeter branched out into real jazz and he was very good. He played "Tunisia Nights". I knew it note for note from my saxophone phase, although my stodgy fingers conjured up more of a wet afternoon in Lewisham than the Maghreb. I slapped my clip board for applause and he bowed.

"Dizzie Gillespie," I said.

"Bravo. You like Miles Davis?" he replied and launched into "So What". A bass and a guitar would have been better than a banjo, but it was still pretty good. Once he had been blond and boyishly good looking. Outdoor work and whatever he took to keep him going through the uncertainties of a busker's life had exacted their toll. But plump trumpeter's cheeks saved him from scrawniness and his eyes lit up when he played. I asked him where he had learned to play jazz.

"Nowhere."

"I don't believe you."

"Why do you want to know?"

"Have you ever eaten in McDonald's?"

"Are you joking?"

"Come on."

The musicians would probably have preferred the money, but curiosity got the better of them. We marched to the head of the queue and, once we had clarified we were going to eat not play, were whisked inside as if on a guest list. We joined the line for one of the thirty serving points and took our trays to a table next to a five-foot-high replica of the Eiffel Tower. I asked the trumpet player again where he had learned to play jazz. As always, you never know how much is true and how much is embellished but, for what it's worth, here it is.

By training Tomas was a musician, piano and trumpet. In the Time of Stagnation he had been in a theatre orchestra and doing a music degree in order to avoid conscription. But the dramaturge, the literary director of the theatre, overheard him playing jazz one lunchtime. The functionary was a political as well as literary commissar and American jazz was officially frowned on. The pillars of socialism trembled before boogie-woogie. Besides, the dramaturge had a nephew who had just graduated from the conservatory at the bottom of his class and needed a job. Tomas was dismissed.

There was nothing standing between him and the army and he was conscripted into a nuclear missile brigade of the Strategic Missile Force in the middle of nowhere, somewhere between Moscow and the Urals. He was older than the other recruits so was not bullied like the school leavers, but he kept quiet about being a musician. Like everyone else, he got by on booze. From the cleaners of the afterburners to the warrant officers who kept the keys to the firing boxes on chains round their necks, they were all perpetually drunk on bootleg vodka.

The base was a secret town, a ZATO – a Closed Administrative Territorial Formation – called Ozyorni-10. In the Time of the Tsars the settlement had been a staging post and railway station for a few large estates. It went into decline after the collectivization of the 1930s and now depended on the missile base for its existence – or its non-existence. It had been expunged from the maps. Not only was it extremely difficult to get to, it was even more difficult to get out of. The roads were guarded. Passes were needed. The only link with the outside was a bus that came and went once a week, usually empty.

The enlisted men came and went as well, but the senior officers and civilians spent their careers in the place. When their children went to university they rarely came back. The soldiers were confined to their barracks near the silos. Senior officers lived in the town. The commanding officer, his deputy, the director of the labs that kept the weaponry alive, the mayor who kept the town functioning, the head of the collective farm that fed everyone – these were the luminaries of the town and their wives were at the pinnacle of social life. Many officers stayed when they retired. A society had developed that Gogol would have recognized, a nineteenth-century garrison town with locals and exiles obsessed with rank, consumed with lethargy and pining for St Petersburg.

The commandant treated the men under his command as serfs. He supplemented his pay by hiring them out to the town and the collective farm. At the beginning of spring, Tomas's platoon was ordered to clean up the gardens and common parts of the apartment block where the élite lived. Tomas was hard at work with a scrubbing brush on the patio when he heard from an open window of a ground-floor apartment the familiar dissonance of the commandant's youngest daughter doing her piano practice. He leaned through the window and gave her advice. Her mother overheard and invited Tomas inside. She sat him down at the excruciatingly tuned piano. The town's piano teacher had died three months before and it had been impossible to find a replacement. The upshot was that the commandant released Tomas from rocketry duties, found him a billet with a widow, Natalya, who had an old wooden house with a garden, and engaged him to teach piano to the children of the town.

Tomas was the envy of his comrades. He joined Ozyorni-10's society, albeit on the lowest rung. He taught piano and singing to children and their mothers, circulating on a bicycle with his music case strapped to the crossbar. When winter came the commandant lent him a driver and a Volga from the car pool. He played music at all the parties. Things went well with the widow Natalya too. He moved from the lodger's attic to the master bedroom. When he was not giving lessons, he helped in the garden in summer and sat by the stove in winter. He liked the town with its old wooden buildings and the high wooden fences round the muddy courtyards. He liked the countryside, the vast open plains, the clumps of trees on the horizon, the placid river with its reeds and herons. As for his music, he stuck to the politically acceptable and never played jazz, even when he was alone. Besides, he could not keep up to date. He did not have a short-wave radio to get Voice of America. He told himself he would wait to catch up when he got back to Moscow and could seek out cafés and cellars and syncopation's other dens. He took no risk of being expelled from his Garden of Eden to the rocket silos.

This pleasant life lasted for almost two years, up to the time of Tomas's discharge from the army. The widow Natalya began to ask over their morning *kasha* what his plans were and insisted on a better answer than "I'll see when I get back to Moscow". His pupils asked what would happen to their lessons and their mothers wondered who would enliven their tea recitals and concerts and parties and play the music for the Komsomol New Year play. All Tomas could do was shrug. It would soon be none of his business.

Three weeks before Tomas's discharge, the commandant told him that there was a problem. Tomas was obliged by military law to complete a minimum number of days of training in things like small arms and map reading, which he had not done. This was very difficult to amend in retrospect, but if he stayed on until the New Year the days could be logged as training days.

From that day on the pressure mounted. The widow doubled her attentions. Tomas was showered with presents after his lessons and recitals. The advantages of provincial life came up in conversation. *It's better to be the first boy in a town than the last boy in a city.* And with pressure came growing revulsion. Natalya's attentions were cloying. His pupils with their wooden fingers and cloth ears bored him with their clockwork sonatas and stupid excuses for not practising. Their mothers were dull and provincial, obsessed with their husbands' rank and what was in the shops today. The town was mouldering and moribund.

Tomas longed for lights and noise and crowded cafés. He loathed the countryside. He hated the wind sweeping across the plain, freezing in winter and dusty in summer. The vast horizon pathetically reflected chronic depression. He was trapped. But what could he do? Insist on his rights? A serving soldier on an island in the middle of the steppe had no rights. The commandant was God. Tomas dared not openly defy him. He had to find a subtle way of making himself undesirable.

His opportunity came one Sunday evening. The commandant and his wife were entertaining their friends around the samovar and Tomas played for them. He sat down at the piano with his back to them and started off with Stravinsky, transcribed for piano from a suite permeated with jazz rhythms. Halfway through he abandoned the score and launched into the Fats Waller that had attracted the dramaturge's malevolence. He was rusty – he had not played jazz for two years. But after a few minutes he warmed to it and was soon so engrossed that he forgot about his audience and the reaction he was banking on: for them to kick this cuckoo of decadence out of their comfortable nest.

He played for nearly half an hour. Fats Waller, Thelonius Monk, Ragtime, Gershwin, all his favourites. Behind him there was silence, not even a cough or the clink of a tea glass. He came to his senses after the final chord of "Summertime". He mopped his forehead with the cuff of his jacket and swivelled on the piano stool to face his listeners. They were turned to wax. They stared at him blankly. He felt a terrible panic welling up from his sandals. What if the commandant had him shot? Packed him off there and then to the Gulag with an instant court martial? He probably had a quorum of officers in the room.

"Is that... jazz?" asked the commandant.

"Yes," said Tomas, lowering his eyes and slumping his shoulders.

"It's wonderful," he said and clapped his hands. All the others started to clap too. The commandant was now on his feet. "Why didn't you play this before?"

"The American pilots in Murmansk played Glenn Miller," said a retired colonel, a grizzled old bear with Brezhnev eyebrows. "We had great parties. Can you play Glenn Miller?" He started to sing and clap. "Da de da de da da. Come on, man. You must know it."

The party at the commandant's lasted until midnight. Tomas played his repertoire three times over before taking a chance on improvising. It was not all jazz. The officers who had been in the Great Patriotic War sang their old songs and told stories about heroic drinking bouts with the Americans and the British and discussed the relative merits of vodka, bourbon, scotch, medical alcohol and engine antifreeze. Their wives clapped along to the rhythm and dragged up the English they had learned at school and showed off decadent western dances they had gleaned from old movies and embellished from their imaginations.

The next day, through the throbbing haze of a hangover, Tomas leaned against an apple tree in the widow's garden and contemplated his new future as the jazz maestro of Ozyorni-10. It wasn't such a bad place, not such a bad life, if he could somehow get hold of US records and sheet music and a radio for Voice of America. The commandant said he could help. He had comrades from the Academy in Berlin and Prague.

Brezhnev died and was replaced by Andropov. Andropov died and was replaced by Chernenko. Chernenko died and was replaced by Gorbachev. The Berlin Wall came down. The Red Army retreated into Russia. In Ozyorni-10 life went on unruffled. Conscripts cleaned the rockets, warrant officers brewed bootleg, the town pursued its social life.

The commandant retired. His replacement had a young Latvian wife who was into Latin American. Tomas built up a combo with drums, sax, guitar, synthesizer. He didn't dare try to find out what his civil status was. He had never received discharge papers and for all he knew he was still a conscript. Or a deserter. His passport was out of date. He could not live or work or marry without those papers. He was a Nobody who lived Nowhere.

In August 1991 Gorbachev's aides tried to oust their boss. Yeltsin stood on a tank outside the White House and defied the coup. In December the Soviet Union died. Yeltsin proclaimed the freedom of the Russian people. Tomas listened to all this happening on the BBC. He orchestrated the New Year's Eve ball and led "Auld Lang Syne" on the trumpet.

The day after New Year's Day he packed up his music and his trumpet and his savings and got on the bus. No one stopped him.

"What do you do without papers?"

"There is a Russian saying. *With papers, you're a human being. Without papers, you're shit.* Do you know free jazz?"

"Sure."

"I am free shit." He grinned.

"Will you play at our opening? I'll get you bowler hats."

Goodness has no smell

Close to where I lived was the church and convent of All Saints. It was a handsome church built in 1733 in the reign of Empress Anna Ivanovna in the muted Moscow baroque style, ochre and white with barely tumescent onions sprouting graceful spires on the belfry and the slate-grey cupola. One snowy Sunday in early winter I went in, enticed by a Russian choir in full voice.

The nave was packed. Incense and mist from damp overcoats and bad breath and fart and mumbled prayer and candle smoke and deep-throated harmonies billowed round the faithful and rose in a reverent miasma to the cupola where Christ Almighty looked down on us, big-eyed and stern and holding his breath.

A murky side-chapel at the back was relatively under-populated, perhaps because two of the worshippers were dead. They lay on their backs in open coffins. Both were old women taking part in their last liturgy, down here anyway, the theory being that they had joined the eternal liturgy up there. One of them, nearer the far wall, was heaped with red gladioli and surrounded by mourners, who said prayers and crossed themselves and bent over to touch the ground and lit candles to stick into trays of sand on brass stands. The other was alone, no flowers, no candles, no mourners. It was so sad. Wasn't there anyone to see her off? The other mourners didn't give her so much as a glance. Nor did the newcomers. They stamped snow off their boots, kissed the icon of the Virgin not two yards from where she lay, lit a candle and crossed themselves three times before pressing forward into the nave.

She was dead. She had no idea she was as friendless now as she probably had been when she was alive. But still, I thought it was a shame. I lurked for a bit in the shadows in front of a faded fresco of the Dormition of Our Lady, cuddling my *shapka* and hoping people would take me for a local. When I felt sufficiently anonymous, I sidled round to the icon of the Virgin and took a fresh candle from the wooden box. The chink-chink-chink of coins was like a gong announcing me. I lit the candle and took it back to the coffin, shielding it with my hand. It was an irrational gesture and I was embarrassed – people might draw the wrong conclusion about who I was. But it didn't seem right for her to be lonely and ignored in a crowd of Christians, even if she were dead.

Her nose was sharp and white and her toothless mouth open in a perfectly round black hole. Her eyes were not quite closed and peeped from under red lids, like my mother pretending to be asleep when I went into her room too early in the morning. Without the benefit of candles or flowers or embalming, the woman exuded the fragrance released when you take the cellophane off a turkey burger that has been out of the fridge too long. She looked like a cross-faced old bitch. Was this why nobody had come to see her off? Once in her life she must have been nice.

Her head was bound in a nunnish wimple and a cheap cotton shroud was laced up to her neck. Her hands were crossed on her breast and her chicken-claw fingers held an ornate ivory crucifix that was at odds with the rest of her pauper's weeds. Her last possession? The one thing she refused to sell? Her candle holder had been appropriated by the popular old woman. I dripped wax on the corner of the coffin and stuck her candle into it. "Good luck darlin'," I whispered and slunk away before the candle fell in the coffin and set fire to her shroud.

Just as I made it to the door, a hand gripped my arm and pulled me back into the shadows of the chapel. I jerked round and saw at my elbow, and no higher than it, a cross-faced old woman, sharp-nosed and toothless. Under a black scarf her head was tightly wrapped in white like a nun. I looked over at the coffin and was relieved to see the dead old woman still in there.

"She knew you'd come," croaked the living crone. She smelt terrible. Not just unwashed but anointed with fetid liniment. I tried to get away, if only from the smell, but she held tight to my sleeve. She pulled me into an alcove where an old man was standing propped against the wall and leaning on two sticks. He wore a long khaki greatcoat and a grubby green woolly hat pulled down over his ears. His yellow parchment face featured bright red scabs that glowed even under a white beard. He had the worst case of the shakes I have ever seen. The poor chap jiggled all over, from nodding head to tapping feet. In a moment of panic I thought the woman was about to introduce me to my putative father. I tried to struggle free, but she held tight. With her other hand she took aim, seized one of his jiggling hands and put it into mine.

"Outside," she rasped and made shooing gestures. Before I could find the words to refuse, she turned away and waddled back into the nave. The shaking man gave me a smile, which immediately turned into a scowl and back into a smile, then a scowl then a smile and so on in an infinite regression of tics. No wonder he dribbled onto his sodden grey scarf. At least he didn't smell as bad as the old woman – unwashed underwear and garlic and damp wool, but no liniment. We processed down the aisle in a manic two-step to the rhythm of his sticks clacking on the floor and every fifth bar or so against each other.

Outside, snow was falling from heaven in thick, wet globs. It got up the nose and in the eyes and slithered down the back of the neck. It dampened the noise of traffic and sirens and people shouting in the street outside. It did nothing against the belfry clanging out the everyday miracle of bread into flesh, wine into blood. Painstakingly we navigated the slippery steps and shimmied down the gauntlet of beggars and collectors rattling their poor boxes like maracas to accompany us.

Once clear in the yard I tried to shake the old man off. "Goodbye. God bless," I said, but he refused to let go of my arm. He lifted a stick and wobbled it in the general direction of a little white building beside the churchyard wall. The stench was unmistakeable. He needed to go.

I breathed through my mouth as I shepherded him up the cement-block steps and across the slippery tile floor to a cast-iron urinal. Thanks for small mercies, he didn't need a crap. He took position and rapped a tattoo on the green-stained iron with his sticks as he fumbled with his flies. There were no buttons or zip, which was a time saver, but he had trouble finding himself in folds of wool and flannel.

"Hold it for me, please," he said.

"Oh Jesus," I said to myself. But I'd gone this far. I reached down and rummaged in the clammy warmth until I found his thing and pulled it out. It was long and wrinkled and covered in red scabs.

"You poor bastard," I said in English and fought down the urge to throw up. Remarkably and conveniently, it was the one bit of him that didn't shake. I held it patiently between thumb and forefinger, trying desperately to think beautiful thoughts, until it gushed a stream of thick yellow soup. When it dribbled to a stop I gave it a perfunctory shake and tucked it back in.

"I meant hold my stick. But thank you anyway," he said.

We skated across the churchyard to a single-storey building built onto the side of the church. Other old people limped and shuffled and staggered with us. The snow was falling thick. I was grateful for the metallic smell of it that killed all others and for the cold that anaesthetized my thumb and forefinger.

In the porch my man rapped on the door with a stick. A spy hole snapped open and shut and the door was swung aside by a nun with brawny bare forearms and an aura of soup. She grabbed him by the shoulders and hoicked him inside. She looked me up and down and without a word slammed the door on me.

The Devil's balls

"**D**zhorn! I have solved all your problems. You will be rich," said Natasha and tinkled like a chandelier in a draught. This was a crystals day when she retuned herself to the cosmos by wearing glittering little bits of glass in her ears, her hair, round her neck, her wrists and pinned all over the front of her blouse. Afanasy warned me not to comment on them unless I wanted the full lecture, including the origin and function of every little shard.

"My cousin is a priest. He has a village and a farm. They will grow everything you need. We will go to him on Saturday and you will give your order."

"But it's snowing."

"The best time. No mud."

It was too good to be true, but there was no harm in checking and it would be a day out. The village was five hours' drive northeast of Moscow in the direction of Nizhny-Novgorod. The engine flogged, the body rattled, and my head banged against the roof as we pounded over the ripples and holes on the motorway. Natasha was hunched over the wheel, knuckles white, her nose nearly on the windscreen, peering through a brown mist thrown up by the trucks. All the vehicles,

★

including ours, were completely stuccoed with it, motorized turds slipping along an open sewer. Roadside petrol stations were unreliable. Like everyone else we were loaded with jerry cans of fuel. If there was a pile-up we would make a glorious firework. The radio didn't work but we couldn't hear it anyway. It was useless trying to talk.

After three hours we turned off the highway onto a local road. Under the snow was a pair of parallel ruts, so at least there was no danger of us sliding into a ditch. Natasha leaned back and relaxed her hands in best Land Rover training school fashion so the wheel didn't break her wrist if we hit a kink in the ruts. The country on either side was a flat white sheet with hummocks of barrack-like buildings.

"Are we nearly there?"

"Nearly there," she said. "That's what you say to children, isn't it?"

"Do you have children?"

"No."

"Are you married?"

"Yes. We couldn't afford a family. Now he sleeps with his professor. I don't see him any more."

"Are you divorced?"

"Of course."

Suddenly she put her foot down and veered to the right. We slithered and tilted and it occurred to me in the lucidity of fear that our conversation had prompted her to escape this miserable life. But she was only escaping the ruts and we fishtailed along a ribbon of packed snow through the forest. It all went quiet, since the engine was almost idling and she only gunned it when we threatened to go broadside.

"We're like the pictures on a Palekh lacquer box. The dashing prince whipping up the sleigh horses and the princess next to him wrapped in furs. Ours is the feminist version."

"Dzhorn! Do all English like empty conversation? It is entertainment for you."

The road spilled out into a clearing. Natasha put her foot on the brake and cut the ignition and we shimmied to a stop in a patch of soft snow. The ticking of the cooling engine was all that remained of the racket of the past few hours. As well as the whooshing in the ears that deep silence brings.

"We're here," said Natasha, a fatuous but customary remark. I wound down the window to see where "here" was. Up to now my view had been through a segment of brown window. Icy breath made me wind it up again fast, but not before glimpsing low wooden houses on the rim of the clearing. They were dark brown and grey and green and hardly visible against the trees beyond them. The giveaway was the curls of smoke and black patches round chimneys on snow-covered roofs.

We bundled our clothes on like lovers in a lay-by. Natasha jumped down nimbly onto the packed snow and made a pirouette. I felt brave and adventurous in the snow-bound wilderness and jumped down less nimbly. My legs shot away from under me and I plumped down on my bottom.

Once bright green and red and blue, the houses had mellowed out of neglect into camouflage colours. Where the wood had rotted they were patched with whatever came to hand: bits of tin, plywood, split logs, tar paper. Piled up around them was the stuff of country life, ramshackle sties and hen houses, bits of old vehicles, privies and dung heaps. In the middle of this rustic slum was a brand new wooden church. Walls of bright yellow plank, roof of rich brown shingles. It was of the old Russian style before it was perverted by onion-dome orientalism and Italian baroque – angular, geometric, cubic, perfectly proportioned. In front was a silver Chevrolet pick-up and a rusty metal caravan with a crooked stovepipe chimney.

I followed Natasha towards the church with the mincing little steps I reserve for walking on snow. The place looked deserted. I suspected eyes behind the curtains. A bearded man slammed the caravan door open from the inside and stepped onto the ammunition box that was his front step. He wore a one-piece scarlet overall tucked into calf-length boots. He opened his arms wide to Natasha and waited for her to get in range to throw them round her. He was only about five foot tall, so he stayed on his box to even things up. They exchanged hugs and smacking-cheek kisses before we made our own, less exuberant acquaintance.

"This is Father Kiril," said Natasha in Russian.

"Cyril, Cyril, Cyril," he said in gangster American. "You from Stateside?"

"England acksherly."

"Okay, okay. The fifty-foist state. Good termeetcha."

Father Cyril was fat in the way weight lifters are fat. Tough with it. He had a bushy black beard and his hair was neatly tied in a bun under a Pittsburgh Steelers baseball cap.

"Yinz must be whacked," he said. "Come inside and drink some hot tea. I got *kasha* on the go."

"Lovely," I said.

The fug inside the trailer was worse than in the Niva. Wood smoke, cooking, ripe trainers, incense. There was just room to huddle on the bed in front of a cylindrical stove. On it was a teapot, a kettle and an encrusted iron saucepan. The bed was the only furniture, nailed together out of un-planed wood, a fakir's treat of splinters and protruding nail heads. A thin lumpy mattress, a matching pillow and a khaki sleeping bag were the only furnishings. Hanging on the wall was an automatic rifle with a skeleton stock. The rest of the cabin was a stash of ten-kilo tins of charity meat, crumbs from the European beef mountain, covered in a jumble of icons and censers and candles and other liturgical paraphernalia. At the end of the bed, covered in transparent plastic, stood a sacerdotal scarecrow made up of a handsome gold-embroidered chasuble and matching hat and stole.

"All your treasures," I said, adenoidally.

"Needs readied up," said Father Cyril. "I'm waitin' on steel doors for the sacristy."

"Black sheep in your flock?"

"It ain't the sheeps I'm worried about, it's the wuffs. There's a military camp about twenty clicks from here.

Soldiers back from Germany. Living in tents, poor guys. They're not bad sonsabitches. They make their own vodka. Drives 'em crazy. Anyways, it's deserters cause the problem. Come spring you'll find plenty bodies out there. If the bears don't find them first. Here. Help yourself to grits."

He gave us tin plates and spoons. I waited for Natasha to serve herself. Thankfully it was not the slimy white stuff but brown and nutty. I took half a spoonful and smeared it round my plate to make it look a lot. Fortunately Cyril was not watching, as he was doing the business with glasses of tea. He handed me one.

"Sugar or sweetener?" he asked, holding up a packet of Sweet'N Low. I chose sugar and regretted it when he passed over a soup bowl of brown sugar. Except it wasn't brown but white coagulated with tea drips.

"So you spent time in America," I said, sipping my unsweetened tea.

"Hey, I was born there. Picksburg."

"I know Pittsburgh," I said.

"You do? Born and raised in the Mon Valley."

It figured. The steel mills along the Monongahela River sucked in immigrants from all over Europe and they brought their religions with them. Driving out from downtown Pittsburgh, past the communities of wooden houses, you see steeples and spires and domes of every rite and denomination from the Atlantic to the Urals.

"How come you're here?"

"My grandaddy was born right here in this village," he said. "He was priest. Got out in the twenties and made it to the Burgh. They wanted to extoiminate us."

"The Bolsheviks?"

"Nope. The New Believers. They were on Lenin's side. Took over our choitches, everything. They got their come-uppance. Lenin turned against 'em too."

"You're an Old Believer?"

"That's what they call us. True Believers if it's all the same to you."

"You still got family in Pittsburgh?"

"Wife and two kids. My Mom's still with us."

"It's amazing how you kept the old faith."

"Only my Grandaddy. That's who I got it from. He never learn English. My Mom and Dad wanted nothing to do with it."

"What do they think of you coming back?"

"My old lady walk out on me when I took up studying for priest. I had a good job at the plant. She didn't take to living on charity. The plant shut down irregardless. Kids arn at school any more. My daughter keeps in touch. She's kept her Russian. Anyways, that's a whole nuther bizniz."

He drained his glass and wiped his mouth with the back of a hairy hand, as if he were trying to wipe the words away too.

"Yinz wanna see the choitch?

We put on our parkas and stepped out into the breath-catching fresh air. Cyril steered Natasha by the elbow and I minced along behind. The sun was setting now over the trees and flooding the clearing with old gold. The church was incandescent.

"Wow, it's like a space ship just landed," I said.

"Nah. They got those ceramic tiles. The re-entry heat bounces offa them. Now you tell me it's a five hunnerd pound ingot just been poured and I might go along wichyer." Mon Valley imagery.

Inside the church was beautiful as an old-fashioned barn. The proportions were delicious. Hidden skylights flooded the steep tent roof with golden light. To the right of the door was an icon with a red lamp burning in front of it and a candle tray with half a dozen guttering candles. The icon was garish and new, Saint Kiril holding a cross and an open bible. He looked remarkably like his priest. Cyril went up to it, crossed himself fluently three times and kissed the foot. He looked pointedly at Natasha.

"Two-fingered heretic," he said in Russian and laughed and clapped her on the shoulder.

"Why two-fingered?" I asked in English.

He was taken aback, surprised that I understood the Russian. "True believers make the sign of the cross with three fingers. For the Holy Trinity. The heretics use two fingers."

"I'm Catholic," I said. "I use four."

"Y'all are a lost cause. At least we got hope with Natasha here. She'll come back. That right, Natasha?"

Before Natasha could think of a suitable reply, the door opened and an old woman came in. She was swathed in black shawls and her feet were swaddled in sacking tied up with parcel string. She shuffled over to Cyril, grabbed his right hand, kissed the hairy fingers and tried to genuflect, much against the will of her arthritic joints. He tried to pull her up with both hands, but she took this as encouragement to subside. They wrestled like this for half a minute until he gave in and let her sink to the floor. She babbled in toothless Russian and Natasha and I diplomatically moved away.

"What's this True Believer stuff?"

"A long time ago in the 1600s the church had reforms. The Old Believers broke away. There are many different sects. This village is *Bezpopovschini*. It means without priests."

"But Cyril is a priest."

"I know, but not like Orthodox. He's not made by a bishop. The people elect him."

"Like our Methodists."

"During the persecutions they lived wild in the forest until it was safe to come back. Villages like this were completely cut off. That's why they have no electricity or roads."

"Or they escaped to Pittsburgh. How did you keep in touch?"

"We didn't. Cyril came to Moscow after *Perestroika*, said his father was my father's cousin. He was trying to find all the people his grandfather talked about. I think he got the wrong family. We have same name, but we never heard of this place and nobody remembers anything about Old Believers."

"Didn't you tell him this?"

"Do you remember the food queues? The best thing in the world was to have was a relative in America. One turns up on your doorstep with dollars in his pocket, you don't send him away."

Cyril gave the old lady a blessing and pulled her to her feet. She backed away from him to the door.

"Did you forgive her sins?" asked Natasha.

"She said someone put the evil eye on her. Yinz got a bed for the night anyways. She keeps a clean house. You won't get bitten too bad."

"Are we staying the night here?" I asked.

"I'm not driving back in the dark," said Natasha.

I was not pleased. There had been no mention of sleeping there. I didn't like her story of acknowledging Cyril just to have an American connection. I could see a long evening ahead with *kasha* and cabbage and home-brewed vodka and a flea-ridden mattress with a priest who wasn't a priest and an old hag with her feet done up in sacking and a batty divorcee, for whom I was just another foreigner who turned up with dollars for the taking. I left them on the pretext of admiring the iconostasis. It was not much to look at: a plain wood partition in front of the sanctuary with a door in the middle underneath a Cyrillic cross. I went up to the door.

"Stay outa there," boomed Cyril.

"What's in there?"

"Nothin," he snapped. "Everythin."

I led the way out of the church and slithered off moodily towards the caravan, while Natasha waited for Cyril to lock up. It was getting dark. I felt cold and fed up.

"Watchat ice, slippy!" shouted Cyril. Too late. My feet shot away from me. I plumped down on my bottom.

The evening was not as bad as I had feared. Our hostess's name was Maria Olegovna. She was probably in her 50s, but thanks to hard work, simple food and the rustic life she looked about 80. From a distance her house was picturesque. Fretwork round the eves, heart-shaped holes in the shutters, a wisp of smoke from a crooked chimney. But we had to tread carefully on the rickety steps up to the balcony and tiptoe round jagged holes in the boards.

Inside was a surprise, bare and spotless, the floor and wooden walls scrubbed white, like a Swedish apartment. Except that in Sweden it indicates post-materialist affluence not pre-materialist poverty. The heat took me by the throat. It came from a massive black-brick stove, a cube with two-metre sides that divided the room in two. On our side were only a couple of benches against the walls, a three-legged stool and a scrubbed pine table covered in a threadbare white cloth. The only decoration was a colour reproduction on shiny cardboard of the *Mona Lisa* in the middle of a white wall. Was there some cross-cultural confusion with the Virgin Mary? On a shelf in the corner next to the door an oil lamp burned in front of a more orthodox icon of Herself.

Maria Olegovna bowed to us and kissed Cyril's hand as if we were living icons come to visit. She had stripped off her shawls down to her best black dress and replaced the sacking on her legs with felt boots, like the elephants' feet you used to put umbrellas in. She protested when I helped carry the benches to the table. Natasha and I sat opposite Cyril. I pointed to Lisa smirking down on us.

"Where did you get the lovely picture?" I asked in Russian.

Maria looked at Natasha, who repeated what I said word for word. She replied to Natasha, who translated for me into English. It was like this all evening. Because I was a foreigner Maria treated me like a half-wit.

"She went to Leningrad when she was a girl. She means Peterburg. A sailor gave it to her."

"I bet he did. Was he a Greek sailor?"

"How should I know? Why do you ask?"

"It's the lid off a box of Greek chocolates."

Cyril asked Maria and for a moment she looked frightened. She gabbled something and scuttled away to the stove.

"She said he was Christian. She means Orthodox. But she could have been saying that for my sake. You nebshit these people, they tell you anything."

There was a taste of bitterness in his remark. It was a hint that his return to the land of his fathers was not quite the prodigal son's homecoming.

Our dinner had more surprises. It was delicious. Several varieties of pickled mushroom, each with a different herb. Wild garlic and tiny eggs, also pickled. Beetroot salad. Smoked pike. Smoked trout. Slivers of smoked wild duck. Nutty black bread.

"This is great. Do they have this every day?"

"Every day a stranger comes to dinner. You're the guest of honour. It's all outa the forest. Eat hearty. You pay a fortune in Moscow for this."

Cyril ate hearty. Natasha picked. I would have preferred cabbage soup. Every mouthful was a reproach made by poverty to affluence. Maria didn't touch the food. She hovered at the end of the table and refilled my plate and watched every bite. For Cyril and me there was vodka to wash it down. It tasted like corn-mash whiskey and was probably made the same way. I looked hard at Natasha aglow in the lamplight, imprinting her on my retinas, in case she was the last thing I saw before I went blind. For Natasha there was a jugful of melted snow. Women don't drink vodka, in public anyway.

"Here's to us," said Cyril, raising his glass. "Welcome to our little corner of the Faith. The early Christians started in the catacombs. Who'd ever believe those guys'd conquer the world? We're the same. Egg-zackly the same. The Tatars drove our ancestors into the forest of Rus. Here we keep the true faith alive. We'll spread out from here. First up, the Babylon of Moscow, ripe for the taking. And when we have the Kremlin then we'll see. You're a lucky man, Johnny, you've seen where it starts. None of us will live to see the end. But we're in at the start. To the Faith!"

We clinked glasses and tossed down the sacramental firewater. While my eyes watered, his were blazing. When I met him I assumed he was cracked. Leaving America to build a church among hovels in the Russian forest I attributed to a sheltered upbringing with a fanatical granddaddy in a Midwest backwater. But now I knew he was more than cracked, he was raving mad. Manic. Messianic.

Succeeding toasts were more cursory and more frequent. Fill – clink – swallow. The food and drink and heat brought euphoria and dizziness. Everyone talking loud. Fill – clink – swallow. Everyone talking soft. Fill – clink – swallow. Rushing in the ears. Fill – clink – swallow. Everything sharp. Fill – clink – swallow. Everything blurred. Fill – clink – swallow. I knew the vodka was really getting a hold when I saw the Devil peeping over the stove, first one side of the chimney pipe and then the other. Pointed head, spiky hair, slant eyes. God help us. A trick of the light. Fill – clink – swallow.

The second course was *kasha*, soft and savoury like couscous. It was smothered in goulash, fibrous lumps hacked off the European beef mountain but tasty nonetheless. I had second helpings in the time-honoured but mistaken expectation that it would soak up the booze. Fill – clink – swallow.

"Natasha," I said, en-un-ci-at-ing every word to stop the sibilants turning into shibilantsh, "it'sh time we dishcushed why we're here."

Blow me if can remember why we're here. The mind's a blank. All I can think of is the old joke about the man who drinks to forget and when he's asked what he's trying to forget says he can't remember. It's so funny I burst out laughing and this fat bloke at the head of the table asks me what I'm laughing at and I tell him and he guffaws too and slaps his thigh and an old lady joins in laughing and the woman opposite looks bored and sips her snowmelt. What's her name? Fill – clink – swallow. Dear God, there's that Devil again.

★

"Dzhorn! I told Cyril you're opening a restaurant in Moscow and that you're looking for farmers to provide the produce."

The woman is looking at me and I don't know what she's talking about. Who the hell is Cyril? Why am I here? I can't even remember where here is. A Pittsburgh bar. An African shebeen. An Irish lock-in. Sure I've been here before. What I don't know is if I ever left. Fill – clink – swallow.

"We got land offa the cooperative. We gotta farm," says the fat bloke. He's got gravy trickling down his beard. Fill – clink – swallow. Fill – clink – swallow. "Tell us what needs growed. We'll grow it."

It's like jogging and bursting through the pain barrier. One minute you feel like you're going to die and the next you feel like you could run for ever. Lucidity is the word. Pure lucidity. The mind is crystal clear even though your speech is not. It's the closest to having a stroke without actually having one. You have to choose your words and be careful not to fall over.

"Potatoes," I said.

"What?"

"Potatoes. I want pot-at-oes." What a ludicrous word. Potatoes. It's the funniest thing I've heard all evening. I laugh, but this time the fat bloke doesn't laugh with me. Better get serious.

"We're starting a restaurant that serves baked potatoes. It's the British answer to pizza. You put stuff like cheese on them. It will really catch on. We do one and then we franchise. First in Moscow then in Peterburg then all over

Russia. Conquer the world. None of us will live to see the end. But we're here at the start."

The fat bloke looks at me like I'm raving mad. Manic. Messianic. "Whaddya want?"

"*Kartoffel*," I say. "*Kartoshka.*"

The old lady stares at me. Her hand is over her mouth like she's smelling her own breath. Over her shoulder is the Devil and this time he doesn't duck down.

"It's a good idea," says the young woman. Natasha's her name, I remember now. Hard to say when you're avoiding shibilantsh. Comes out Natasa. The fat guy, Shyril's his name, looks as if he's going to burst a blood vessel. His face is crimson.

"Devil's food," he says.

"We're not talking dessert here," I say. "Main course. *Kartoffel.*"

"*Kartoffel* is the filthy German word. The true Russian name is *gulba*. You know what it means? It means going astray. Sin. It's the forbidden fruit Adam and Eve ate."

"You're thinking of apple. You know, apple for the teacher."

"Tayder is the Devil's apple. Whoever eats it disobeys God, violates the Holy Testament and will never inherit the Kingdom of Heaven."

"Shorry Shyril. We're talking potatoes here. There are no potatoes in the Bible."

"Outa your mouth you said it. It ain't food for Christians."

"Of course it's not in the Bible. It hadn't been discovered yet. The prophets were good but not that good."

"You blaspheme."

"Shorry. Sor-ry."

"The tayder was the incarnation of the evil thing."

I look over to Natasha for help. She has her hands over her eyes. I'm on my own.

"Didn't you ever eat French fries in Pittsburgh? Mashed potato and gravy?"

"Food for unbelievers."

"But they eat potatoes all over Russia."

"The evils of Russia come from tayders. You know how they wiped out leprosy in Siberia? They stopped eating tayders. You know the cure for syphilis?"

"Crisps?"

"Tayder. Same family as deadly nightshade. Taste its leaves. Bitter poison."

"There's your mistake, Cyril. You don't eat the leaves. You eat the root bit."

"And what happens? Wind and lust. Wind and lust."

"Hey, go easy. Those are my hobbies."

Natasha still has her hand over her eyes. I'll kill her. She must have known this maniac had a thing against potatoes. She dragged me out here for a sick joke.

"You know what we call this tayder a yours."

"*Gulba.* You said. Going astray."

His voice drops and his eyes burn into mine and spittle trickles from the corner of his mouth. "*Shari Diavolu.* The Devil's balls."

What can I say? I'm choking down a laugh. Maria crosses herself and scampers back to the stove.

The rest of the meal was rather subdued. So that's why there was *kasha* with everything. I should have spotted what was missing from the menu. I could have understood it from the mouth of some ancient peasant, but this drivel from a man I could have sat next to on the 137 Shadyside Express? At Three Rivers Stadium? On a bar stool in the Wheel Café? Ancient superstitions persecuted from the Old World into the New, to be nurtured there for generations and brought back on a 747.

Pudding was tinned peaches and evaporated milk. Then a heavy sponge cake smeared with jam. And tea. Natasha made small talk about lettuces and beetroot and other Christian things they could grow for us on the farm. Like a thunderstorm on the Steppes, Russian rows fade away as fast as they spring up. Fill – clink – swallow.

When we finished eating Cyril blessed us all, made his obeisance to the icon in the corner by the door, put on his parka and baseball cap and went out into the night. I admired the straight line he walked. When I went round the corner for a pee on the dung heap I had to hold on to the wall. For a moment I was uncertain whether the icy air would sober me up or strike me unconscious, but I survived.

Natasha helped Maria clear the table while I sat on a bench and took deep breaths and practised focusing on the Mona Lisa and exercised my curiosity about the sleeping arrangements. It was satisfied when Natasha appeared from behind the patchwork curtain beside the stove and beckoned to me.

"Dzhorn! Bedtime," she said.

Navigating by the wall, I joined her. Behind the curtain was an alcove made by the wall, the stove and another curtain. Filling the alcove was an enormous bed, more than a double, a triple, a bridal bed with carved headboard and pillars at each corner and a mountain of grey quilt and off-white sheets and a bolster with a lacy cover. Natasha stood on the other side of the bed in her blouse and knickers, her chestnut hair billowing over her shoulders. She looked at me with eyes made moist and mellow by the faint light from the little oil lamp on top of the stove. She was smiling. There was tenderness and mischief in her smile.

"I'm sorry about tonight," she said, rolling back the quilt to get in. "I didn't know." She lay on her back looking up at the wooden ceiling. I fumbled off trousers and shoes and socks. On the other side of the curtain I heard Maria blowing out the oil lamps. It all went dark.

I slid under the quilt. The rough and prickly patchwork sheet had not quite made the transition from vegetable to fabric. It felt like beaten straw. I lay still until the bed stopped spinning. I thought it was polite to give Natasha a goodnight cuddle and quite safe, as it was all I was capable of. I rolled on my side and stretched out my arm and caressed a hard, bony body in a shell of coarse material. A rough-skinned talon gripped my wrist and pushed me away.

"Goodnight, Maria," said Natasha. She couldn't keep the laughter out of her voice.

"Good night, God spare us," croaked the bony thing next to me.

I lay back rigid on the bolster. My eyes got used to the dark. In the faint red glow from the icon lamp I saw the Devil peering down at me from the top of the stove.

"*Shari Diavolu!*" I shouted and sat bolt upright.

"It's my son," said Maria. "Dimitri. He's a good boy."

He had a man's body and a tiny pointed head. He squatted on top of the stove with a blanket round his shoulders. I waggled my fingers at him, the only greeting I could think of. He pulled the blanket round him and lay on his side, still looking down at us. The last thing I remember was wondering if the Greek sailor's name was Dimitri.

I have very little recollection of the next morning. Not exactly a hangover, but the feeling that my brains had turned to hot *kasha* and were about to burst out of my ears. Dimitri was nowhere to be seen. Cyril was tough and hearty, as if he had spent the night on lemonade. I took little sips of tea and fudged through the haze of farewells. I managed to get to the Niva without plumping down on my bottom.

"Dzhorn! I'm sorry," said Natasha as we slalomed down the forest track. "I didn't know about the potatoes. It is the truth."

"Not to worry," I said. "It's given me a great idea for a Jackets Special. *Shari Diavolu.*"

How to avoid vampires

I t was a glorious spring day. The breeze was from the south. The snow had gone from our square. Leafless trees and yellow turf were pricked with emerald. I needed a holiday.

I hurried from the station to the forest as if I was late for an appointment. Since I find no pleasure in snow, it was the first time I had been in the woods for nearly six months. I wandered through the trails, deliberately getting lost, shucking off city air and city concrete and city noise and city straight lines. Leaves and roots and bark and mud were equally delicious. Birds squabbled in the undergrowth and chattered and sang. I succumbed to the urge to join in the warbling. ♪*There were birds in the trees, but I never heard them singing...* ♪

There were other people. Mothers and grandmothers with children, still swaddled as if it were 15 below. One young mother navigated an old-fashioned perambulator entirely unsuitable for the terrain, utterly immersed in the lullaby she crooned to the bundle of pink wool under the canopy. I felt bountiful and wished I was a good fairy and could give the child a present – the knack of two-fingered whistling, a talent for the ukulele, a visa for America – but all I had to bestow was a benevolent smile. Couples with eyes only for each other strolled decorously, wondering perhaps if the ground behind the bushes was still too damp. A white-haired veteran in an ancient suit with a chest full of medals stared into the tree tops and savoured victory over another winter.

I pushed on down narrower and narrower trails, skipping over logs and muddy bits. The narrow path ended in a clearing. In the middle was a round pond covered in dead leaves and green sludge. There was a bench made of logs and I was disappointed that two men were sitting on it. One was about my age, very gaunt, in a black serge suit and black polo-neck. I suspected he had a wasting disease, because his hair was sparse and lifeless and his skin pale and leathery and his eyes sunk in dark sockets. The other man was young, perhaps late teens, with bouffant black hair and the wisp of a first moustache. He wore black jeans and a brown leather jacket. They each held a piece of manuscript paper and sang to each other in soft bass voices.

They stopped and looked at me with theatrically raised eyebrows. My first impulse was to turn round and go back the way I had come. They looked so harmless and at the same time so sinister that I was in two minds. Curiosity won out. I sauntered towards them and nodded, po-faced, Russian style. They turned back to their manuscripts and start singing again. I ignored them and gazed into the filthy pool with my hands in my pockets.

♪*What does he see… he see… he see?"*♭

The only way out of the clearing was the way I had come. I waved my hand cheerily and made for the path, but Bouffant stood up and in a couple of strides blocked my way. His speaking voice was a flat monotone. "Please join us."

"Yes, join us," growled Gaunt, more an order than an invitation.

"You're musicians," I said.

"Poor singers..."

They laughed for the first time and start their recitative again, this time led by Bouffant. ♪*We're singers... poor singers are we... poor singers... do join us...*♪

It was stupid to be nervous. What was there to fear from musicians? Besides, they could be interesting. An early bluebottle, still sluggish from winter, drifted onto my cheek and I slapped it away. Bouffant copied my movement and slapped his own cheek. I went with him to the bench and Gaunt pointed to the place beside him. I sat down and Bouffant sat on the other side of me.

"It's a nice day," I said.

♪*Nice day... nice day... nice day... nice day.*♪ They went down a minor scale and ended on a discord.

"Was that a Doric scale?" I asked, dredging up memories from an improvisation class when I was infatuated with the saxophone. I didn't know which one to look at so I stared at the pool. Midges hovered over the slime. Gaunt put a bony hand on my knee. I tried to edge away, but Bouffant was up close to me. I could smell his peppermint breath and feel it on the back of my neck. I tried to stand up, but Gaunt's hand pressed down.

"Are you with an opera?"

"Opera is dead. Theatre is dead. Concert is dead," growled Gaunt.

"We make our own music," said Bouffant.

"You have fine voices."

They broke into a syncopated scat, really very good. In normal circumstances I would have enjoyed it. ♪*Bum-chi-cha-cha... bum-chi-cha-cha... katashawawa katashawawa...*♩

Gaunt in my right ear, Bouffant in the left. I joined in, a light baritone. ♪*Shagashagashaga.*♩

Bouffant now had my left elbow and I realized I was pinioned, gently but firmly. I decided not to attempt to break out in case it led to something worse. Gaunt may have been wasting away but his fingers were strong. I tried to get to my feet, but they squeezed my arm and my thigh. I struggled, but Gaunt reached over his body and gripped my free arm with his free hand. I was pinioned. Now I was seriously afraid. I looked round over my shoulder, but there was no one coming down the path.

"What do you want?" I asked, no longer a light baritone but a tremulous tenor. They broke into song again.

♪*Bum-chi-cha-cha... bum-chi-cha-cha... katashawawa katashawawa.*♩

"Let me go!"

"No, my friend. Deeper. Like this... ♪*Let me go... let me go...*♩

Humour them, humour them. But my voice can't get down so low. "Let go my arm. Take my purse."

Bouffant slid his free hand inside my coat, took out my wallet and slipped it inside his leather jacket. They let go of my arms and I was halfway to my feet when they took hold of my coat collar and pulled it down my back, so my arms were pinioned again and I fell down on the bench. I yelled for help at the top of my voice. I shoved hard and jerked and came free from my coat. I lunged and staggered towards the pond.

When I got to the edge I jumped. Straightened my legs and touched bottom. Thick mud. It was too shallow to swim and I splashed into the middle. I turned and waited for them. The water was up to my knees, then up to my thighs as I sank into the mud. The men walked round the edge of the pool in opposite directions. It was icy cold. I started to shiver.

♪*Let him drown.* ♭

Bouffant laughed. They shambled to the path. They looked back at me.

"You'll get pneumonia," said Bouffant.

"Why don't you sing?" said Gaunt. "It will keep you warm."

"Sod off!" I shouted.

They disappeared into the trees singing, Bouffant taking the melody and Gaunt in simple thirds. They grew fainter, but I didn't trust them. They might have been hiding behind a diminuendo. I could feel my feet in the squelching mud but nothing above the knees. I waited until the cold reached my chest before wading to the edge.

Hunkered down with my arm round my knees in a pathetic attempt to keep warm, I waited to jump back into the pool. When I was more terrified of hypothermia than meeting them again, I made a run for it. Bastinadoed by roots and nettles, whipped by briars and branches, painted all over with green algae, I staggered down the path, bent double with cramp. Lost and disoriented, I chose the widest path at each crossroads.

Soon I met other people, but I gave up shouting for help – they ran away faster than me. One small boy was transfixed by the apparition of the green man until he was swept up by his father. I jumped up and down and beat my arms until I didn't drip any more and headed for the metro. Thank goodness I had a token and loose change in my pocket. In the safety of the carriage, I realized that I had left one of my new Russian shoes at the bottom of the pond. I had cuts and bruises all over my foot.

I'd been mugged before by children in Rome, on the beach in Dar es Salaam, in the kasbah in Casablanca. This was my first experience of grown-ups, musical muggers at that. For some time afterwards I had an aversion to male-voice choirs, walks in the forest and puree of spinach.

Wake in the night. Headache. Shivers. Sweats. Dizzy. Chest pain.

Is this it?

IT?

Lie still. It will pass.

More pain. Please no.

IT.

Dear God… Our Father… Hail Mary…

Daylight atheist. Death-bed reversion.

Phone home. Say goodbye. Love you all.

It'll worry them. It'll worry me.

Phone the doctor. Which doctor?

Phone the hospital. Which hospital?

What is Russian for poorly? What is Russian for help?

Attacked in the street don't shout "Help!" Shout "Fire!"

Do that down the phone they send a fire engine.

Call an ambulance. What number? It's two digits.

Different ones for each emergency.

04 is a gas leak.

Oh God. My Russian's gone.

Astarozhne. Stanzie akrivaetse.

Attention. Station approaching.

All I can remember.

Travel insurance. Where did I put it?

I'll be dead by the time I get through.

Used them before. Treat you like a malingerer.

Broken leg? Snap out of it. Try hopping.

Insurance. Lovey-dovey when they want your premium.

Treat you like a criminal when you need them.

Stop ranting. Do something.

Clean underpants. Don't want them to find me in these.

Ambulance is 01. No, that's fire.

No idea how it all works. Never bothered to find out.

In England you have to stagger out into the street.

Ambulances don't come to the house.

20 below outside.

Oh God help me. I'm sorry. Won't do it again.

What are you sorry for?

I dunno. Anything you like, God. Just help me.

Will they take me home? Or bury me in Novodevichy.

I'm burning. Bed's on fire. Smoking in bed.

Water. Get water in the kitchen.

Where are my feet? Those aren't my feet.

They're someone else's feet.

Who stole my feet? Muggers. Bastards.

Use them anyway. Get up. Agony. Stagger.

Doorpost to sofa to table to fridge.

Don't turn on light. Eyes hurt.

Crunch on cockroaches. Goo between the toes.

Nice and cool. Dark in the fridge. Nothing in it.

Shit. It's the oven. Where's the fridge?

No. That's the microwave.

Where am I? Talk to me someone.

No don't. Don't hallucinate.

Jerk open the oven. A burst of light.

Oh my eyes. It's the fridge.

Chablis. Vodka. San Pellegrino. Caviar.

Big green turd. No roaches.

Swig off the Pelly.

Bubbles up the nose. Dribble down the chin.

Chest pain grows. Big burp. Chest pain goes.

Cold sweat. Hot shivers.

Mummy, I'm poorly. Make it better. Mummy.

Take out big green turd. Bread knife.

Thick slices in the light of the fridge.

Grab the Pelly. Stagger to sofa.

Crash.

Cover eyes and face with slices of gherkin.

Cool. Good for the complexion. What a way to go.

Salmon on a buffet covered in cucumber.

Diving. Down. Spinning. Down the maelstrom.

Down the plughole. Am I going clockwise or anticlockwise?

Black hole. DON'T GO DOWN THERE!

Come back.

Great swig of fizzy water. And another.

Fight back. I'm here, Mum.

They're my own feet now. Muggers sent them back.

Tickle and prickle. Up the ankles. Up the calves and shins.

I know what it is. I am calm. I am alive. I know what it is.

On my hands. Up my arms. Into the armpits.

On my belly and chest and neck and round my face.

Nibbling at the gherkin. In my hair. Foraging in dandruff.

Cockroaches.

Tickling feelers. Scratching feet. Pricking mandibles.

Big black juicy cockroaches. Full of goo.

On the floor, in the carpet, a sea of cockroaches.

The sofa an island of cockroaches.

My body a mountain of cockroaches. Heaving.

Scratch and nibble. Scratch and nibble.

All over me. Roaches.

I'm covered in cockroaches.

Can't move.

Turn on a light, they scuttle and are gone.

Don't do that. Eyes hurt.

Feet will squidge and crackle them.

Bear it. Bear the pain. Bear the weight.

Pounds of cockroaches.
Cockroach on cockroach on cockroach.
Hands on my ears. Eyes and mouth tight shut.
Ache and shiver and tingle with cockroach.
Oh Mum. I'm so far from home.

Twenty-four hours and it was gone. The roaches scattered. There was rustling behind the cupboard and in the garbage chute, but no sight of the buggers other than the wrecks I had trodden on.

There was another bottle of Pelly in the fridge – I downed it in one go. I found a heel of black bread and a tin of sprats and took them into the bedroom with the nub end of gherkin left over from my face pack. I looked in the mirror. Puffy face, eye bags, a rash of tiny spots, cockroach kisses. I changed my clothes, damp with feversweat. I ate the sprats, skin and bones. I didn't care, slurped the last bit of acrid sauce from the tin, gnawed the bread, chewed the gherkin, rind and all, and fell into a dreamless sleep.

The next morning I woke up better but exhausted. It was Saturday. I phoned Flor but must have misdialled, because Natasha answered. She sounded alarmed when I described my symptoms. She offered to bring me food and I did not refuse. I hardly had the strength to go to the bathroom, so shopping was out of the question. I made tea and slept in three-hour cycles until she arrived.

Flor came too. They looked at me with the sympathy and revulsion you feel for the old and sick. A third person was with them, a big-boned, middle-aged woman in an

★

ankle-length black-leather coat and a Cossack fur hat, angular face and lidded black eyes and purple lips and a single eyebrow from ear to ear, a villain from a Marvel comic. I was glad I didn't meet her in the middle of my fever. Roachwoman. She took me in with a glance, spat me out and marched into the living room. She was the first visitor not to be impressed. She inventoried the Western fixtures and fittings with a stony stare while Flor dipped into one of the shopping bags for a turnip and a jar of honey.

"This is Udmurt medicine. I will scoop out the middle and fill with honey. After one night, you drink the honey in tea."

"Gee thanks, Flor. I feel better already. What do I do with the turnip?"

"This is my friend Ivana Ivanovna," said Natasha. "She is doctor."

We shook hands and exchanged the usual glum greetings. She looked at me as if I had three months to live and it was my own fault.

"Tell her I'm over the worst."

Ivana Ivanovna took off her hat and coat to reveal a calf-length black-leather dress and a cap of black hair swept back and into a tight bun. She looked me up and down and stared at a point over my head. I looked up, but the only thing of interest was a ceiling tile coming loose.

"She says to tell exactly what is wrong."

"I suddenly got a fever in the middle of the night. And it suddenly went away. I've got a bit of a sore throat. And these spots. I feel very tired. I'm sure I'll be fine in a couple of days."

Ivana Ivanovna shrugged her shoulders. She did not examine me, open your mouth and say aaah, let's hear your chest. Not even a thermometer. She just looked at me like Cruella de Vil sizing up a puppy. Unable to stand any longer, I slumped on the sofa.

"It's nothing. I was in a pond yesterday. I must have caught a chill."

"Dzhorn! Why were you in pornd?"

My Russian had evaporated with the fever. Natasha interpreted while Ivana Ivanovna chuntered next to her. As I told the story of my mugging and heroic escape, she became more and more interested, eyes unlidded and eyebrow arched. I knew what she was thinking. I had caught some horrible disease from the stagnant water. But I hadn't swallowed any and I'd showered as soon as I got home. It was just a chill. Ivana Ivanovna said something to Natasha that made her blanch. Both of them looked at me as if I was contagious.

"Dzhorn! I have bad news. You must not be afraid."

"Oh dear."

"You have been attacked by vampires."

"What?"

"Vampires. Those men yesterday. They suck from you."

"They didn't touch me. They didn't take anything. They took my wallet."

"Yes, they steal from you. They take what they want."

"How? I've got no bites. No teeth marks."

It shows how exhausted I was that I didn't laugh but carried on this ridiculous conversation.

"Dzhorn! These are not blood vampires. We do not have blood vampires in Moscow."

"One less thing to worry about."

"These are *energeticheskiye vampir*."

"Better than lazy ones."

"Dzhorn! You have bad thoughts. You are full of mocking. She says you are definitely victim."

"Victim of what?"

"Energy vampires. They suck energy out of you. Out of your mind and out of your body. This is why you are tired."

"Rubbish. It's a virus."

"You see? You attack me. Doesn't he attack me, Flor?"

Flor shrugged and studied the bookcase. I lay back on the sofa. Ivana Ivanovna stood by my side and held her hands, palms down, about three feet over my head, with her eyes closed. I didn't have the strength to tell her to go away. Besides, it was a good story for later. After several minutes she turned away and sat down on a dining chair, hands on her lap. She seemed in a better mood, almost chatty as she gave her full diagnosis for Natasha to translate.

"They have attacked all your auras. Your purple aura is severely damaged. This is why you are exhausted and with mental problems. You will sleep badly and have bad dreams and waking dreams. She says your red aura is harmed too. Do you have problems at the toilet? The green is only slightly touched, which is good about your heart."

"What is all this about?"

"All people have seven auras like rainbow. Energy vampires steal from them. Sickness comes in the parts of the body fixed to the aura that they suck. Last year I was attacked in the yellow aura and had problems with liver."

"How does she know my auras are damaged?"

"Oh Dzhorn! She can see them. She can feel them in her hands."

For the first time since I had woken up with the fever, I felt truly frightened. Not about the taradiddle of my auras, but frightened that I was having a hallucination. It felt so real. The disorientation of Russia, the stress of trying to achieve something, the mugging… yet if I was having a breakdown would I realize I was having it? Isn't fearing you are going mad a sign of sanity?

"Your chakra is open to life force of the cosmic rays but it is closing. Dzhorn! You are in grave danger. You have no energy to keep it open. If it closes then you will have no more energy. You will become vampire too. You must steal life from other people."

"I said they didn't touch me."

"They have invisible pipe from their chest. They put it into your aura and they suck. They do not need to touch your body."

This was such tripe. Humour them. "How do I get better?"

"Ivana Ivanovna is psychic doctor. She will cure you. She has many successes."

"Wonderful."

"You must pay her."

My throat hurt when I laughed. Everyone had something to sell. But it was worth it. Hard cash would prove if she was a hallucination.

"How much?"

"Ten dollars. With massage."

Hallucination or not, a massage from a woman in a leather dress and purple lipstick would be difficult to explain when I got home. But worth the trouble. "Go on then."

"Money first. Massage after."

I hobbled into the bedroom for my wallet. Ivana Ivanovna followed. I gave her the tenner and was disappointed that she didn't tuck it into her cleavage. I was embarrassed by the bed, sweaty and crumpled. She nodded to it and I lay down. I waited for the towels and unguents and instructions to undress.

There is the medical massage, the sports massage, the parlour massage. They all offer relief in their own way. And then there is the psychic massage. This offers no relief to the psychically insensitive, indeed no sensation at all. The masseuse waves her hands over the body of the massee and about three inches above it.

"Turn over, please," she said in Russian.

"What? Is that it?"

I rolled on my stomach and she continued to massage my auras. She could have been polishing her nails or inspecting her split ends for all I knew.

"Dzhorn! You must drink this," said Natasha, coming into the bedroom. I sat up and she handed me a Father Christmas mug steaming with a black liquid smelling of coffee.

"What is it?"

"It is good medicine. Drink."

Russian bedside manner is the old fashioned do-as-you're-told variety. I did as I was told. It was instant coffee with a strange taste. "What is in this?"

"Coffee and a big spoon of pepper. You must drink this every morning before you leave the house and when you come back in the evening. And you must have cold shower. And you must quickly dance like this."

She jogged and flapped her hands up and down. Ivana Ivanovna interrupted her.

"She says you must sit in the morning after your coffee and imagine you are in the middle of an egg made of gold. This will protect you. You must play soothing music and feel the harmony of nature. If you go on the grass you must walk barefoot and you should embrace the trees."

I was waiting for crystals. Crystals had to come into it somewhere.

"For ten dollars she will find right crystal for you."

Vegetarianism would be next. That was OK. In Russia a vegetarian is someone who eats meat only once a day.

"You must not eat meat. Or see pornography. Rock music is bad and science fiction movies. This apartment is full of bad things. Ivana Ivanovna thinks the owner is a vampire. All these things imported from the West suck energy from Russian soul. Video games and guns and movies and computers. She believes you are in danger."

"Thank her for the warning. I will watch out for psucking psychic psyphons."

"She will call you when she has found right crystal."

★

They let themselves out. Laughter may not be the best medicine, but I did feel better that evening.

Up to now the covers on the bookstalls in the street that caught my eye had been pornography and thrillers and horror and sci-fi. But now I noticed the proliferation of sober little self-help manuals with titles like *Ten Steps to Defend Against Energy Vampirism* and *How to Avoid Vampires*.

Flor had a better theory. He said that the Bolshoi had its own psychiatric hospital until it was closed when state funding dried up. I took to black coffee with pepper, just in case, and it made dire Russian instant slightly more palatable.

Gorky Park

For a time I was nervous about walking in the woods, but I thought Gorky Park was safe enough. Many people have heard of Gorky Park, if only because of the thriller and the film. It's an amusement park on the south bank of the Moscow River, fun if you like rides and attractions. Less well known is the oldest part of the park, the Neskuchny Gardens that run southeast along the river down to Gagarin Square, 250 acres, some of it natural woods and some laid out with alleys and sculptures and ponds.

One warm Thursday afternoon I decided to walk the length of the gardens and through Gorky Park to get over my fear of mugging and to work up a thirst for Sally O'Brien's, which had just opened. It was about three miles, so I reckoned I would earn my pint. I had gone about a mile when ahead of me I caught up with a young couple, he in a cape and wizard's hat, she in a leather jerkin and long-tailed pixie hat. The pixie chanted in a monotone while the wizard strummed a mandolin. Their aura of mystery was diluted by the pixie's plastic bag clanking with bottles. They looked daft but harmless.

I followed them down a side path and into a clearing, where a score of other people in various stages of fancy dress

⭐

lolled on tables and benches made of tree trunks. They were in their late teens, early 20s, mostly young men, and it was obvious that the party had already started. A big man with a red beard and a Laplander's hat waved a bottle at me and shouted to come and join them. Never one to turn down the offer of a beer, I sat on a vacant stump beside him.

"Where are you from?"

"England."

"Mmmm," hummed the people around me as Red-Beard flipped the top off a bottle of Zhiguli and handed it to me. Bottled beer was not cheap. These were middle-class kids, probably university students.

Before we could follow up the introductions, a blonde waif in a long flowing dress stepped out into the middle. She started to sing in a small, clear, pure voice, unaccompanied. We all stopped guzzling and talking to listen. The tune sounded Russian, but I couldn't decide whether it was a folk tune or an improvisation. The words were certainly not Russian. I thought they might have come from one of the northern peoples, a Finnish dialect perhaps. She looked lovely against the trees, backlit now by the sinking sun. She finished and there was an enchanted moment of silence before we applauded and she went back demurely to her tree trunk.

"That was beautiful," I said to Red-Beard. "What language was it?"

"Sindarin, of course," he said.

"Where's that from?"

There are about 70 different minority ethnic groups in the Former Soviet Union speaking about 170 different

271

languages and dialects, so it was not surprising to me that I hadn't heard of Sindarin. It was to him, though. He looked at me glassy-eyed, from beer or astonishment, and followed it with a burp of less doubtful provenance. He switched to English. "You are English? You do not know? It is Elven-tongue."

"Song of the Eagle," said the lad next to him, a fresh-faced youth in a hat that made him look like a pantomime village idiot, although I suspect this wasn't the effect he was striving for.

"Your greatest English writer. The Master."

"Ahh, Shakespeare," I said, back on firm ground and struggling to remember the play featuring the Song of the Eagle.

"Dzeh Air Air Tolkien," Red-Beard intoned. They were looking at me now with suspicion and dislike. I was an interloper, an impostor, at best an ignoramus. The last of these is certainly true where Tolkien is concerned. Good yarns, but that's far as it goes. As for mugging up on his mythologies and languages, there are not enough hours in the day for real-world ones, which I find a lot more interesting than his donnish fabrications. Now was not the time to say so, though.

"Oh yes. Tolkien. I knew his son."

This changed the mood. Everyone within hearing perked up.

"You knew family of Tolkien?"

"His son taught me Latin." He also took us for Catholic Prayers, an annoying innovation in my fourth year that

★

replaced larking around in the gym or finishing homework while the Prods were in assembly.

"Oh God. He made *The Silmarillion*."

I had never met Christopher, who edited the ragbag of Middle Earth mythology he inherited. My schoolmaster was his elder brother, Michael, but I hadn't the heart to put them right. He was a nice man, world-weary, I-wish-I-was-doing-something-else-but-this-is-what-I-do-best. Red-Beard took my hand and held it, as if the life force of the Great Fabulist somehow ran through the genes and had lingered all these years on my palm. I changed the subject.

"I grew up in the same place as Dzeh Air Air Tolkien."

There were sighs and murmurs of approval. "Is that the Shire?"

"One of them. There are several. Ours was the Shire of War-Wick. In the middle of England."

"Middle Earth."

"We natives call it the Middle-Lands."

By now they had all gathered round me in a circle. I felt obliged to give them something. I dug out a piece of trivia that my friend Andrew Stephens, who lived in Edgbaston, had told me on top of a number 35 bus. "You know the Two Towers?"

"Of course," they chorused in Russian and English and Elvish.

"They are inspired by the towers of the Edgbaston Water Works."

They took this news without flinching and got into a heated debate about whether the Two Towers were Minas this or Minas that or Minas the other. I took the opportunity to slip away. I didn't feel I could sponge another Zhiguli and the sun was going down. We clinked bottles in farewell.

"You are always welcome to Eglador," said Red-Beard. "Every Thursday afternoon."

I solemnly shook hands with everyone and with Sindarin farewells left the park. It was too late to walk all the way to Sally O'Brien's, so I got the metro.

I tried to remember if hobbits ate potatoes, but they were anachronistically New World. Nevertheless, Bilbo might have when he took ship for the West with the Elves. A Bilbo Special on the menu, then.

Natasha told me disparagingly that these people were Tolkienuti, conveniently translatable as Tolkien Nuts. Eglador was the name of a Tolkienian kingdom. If I was growing up in New Russia I might have taken refuge in an Eglador too. I never went back there. I heard that later the fantasy world degenerated into violent battles between drunken young men dressed up as Orcs and Trolls and that the police suppressed it.

We must pay now

I thought I had heard the last of Andrei Denisovich and his pantacrene and sea shells, but one day he telephoned to say that he wanted to meet me urgently. He suggested the Aurora Hotel. In the Time of Stagnation it had been a hotel for officials of the Union of Inland Navigators.

The walls, floors and ceilings of the public spaces were clad in brown marble streaked with yellow. Andrei was sitting in an alcove in front of a map of the Volga inlaid in red marble mosaic, a river of blood. He was wearing a dark business suit, which made his unhealthy pallor more livid and a vodka flush more angry. When he stood up to meet me he looked over my shoulder and then to his right and left. There was only one other person in the room, a grey-haired man in shabby clothes reading a newspaper. He looked left over from the old days, certainly not a New Russian.

Although I had learned not to smile when meeting it still felt odd, as if we were here to exchange bad news. We sat down awkwardly on the edges of our chairs and Andrei glanced over my shoulder to the door. We ordered coffee from a swarthy waiter and got down to business. He took a file out of a plastic crocodile-skin briefcase.

"We now have feasibility for Barents Sea."

"Sorry, Andrei. Our board has finalized our strategic plan. There's no place for sea shells."

His ears twitched back, his furrowed forehead cleared, his eyes narrowed and for a split second he was a Tatar.

"We have found dredger. Special sea-shell dredger. Here is offer."

"Sorry, Andrei, my board's decided. What can I do?"

It felt strange being on the receiving end. It was usually my crackpot ideas getting the brush-off. The flash of the Tatar again. Andrei looked right and left and over my shoulder. The swarthy waiter set down our coffee.

"Fireworks. We have ship of fireworks in St Petersburg harbour. Certified by Russian authorities. Ready to sail. Five thousand dollars downpayment. Russian fireworks are the best. You have fireworks in England?"

"Fifth of November."

"Not fourth of July?"

"Fourth of July is somewhere else."

"They will keep to November."

"I'll take it to my board but I don't hold out much hope, Andrei."

"Wolfram. We have licence to prospect wolfram in Kazakhstan. It is biggest wolfram concession in Soviet Union."

"What is wolfram?"

"For light bulbs. Very hard metal. Also for warheads."

"Tungsten? You have a licence for tungsten?"

"One final payment and we have it."

"Five thousand dollars?"

Andrei shrugged. He took a slug of coffee. His hands were shaking. All the blood in his face had drained to the red blobs on his cheeks.

"Two thousand dollars. I have the papers with me. Two thousand."

He took out a sheaf of onion-skin papers, closely typed and smudged. He held them out to me, but I did not take them. I was no longer entertained by this poor Russian Tatar. I felt sorry for him. Sea shells, fireworks, tungsten. Three more for the list of improbable dreams touted in hotel lobbies all over Russia.

"What do you really want, Andrei? Why do you need two thousand dollars so badly?" This is what I wanted to say, but I didn't want to get involved. It would be cruel to string him along.

"Take the papers," he said quietly. "One thousand dollars."

"They mean nothing to me, Andrei."

He looked hard over my shoulder. His shoulders sagged and he slumped back in his chair, the papers quivering in his lap. He looked over my shoulder again and I turned round, but the lobby was empty. He was desperate, but it was not my problem. I finished my coffee and stood up. He stood up too, laboriously, leaning on the table for support.

"I will come with you," he said, throwing the papers in his briefcase and slamming it shut. We came out of the alcove. The lobby was deserted. He looked about him right and left. He gripped my arm and steered me towards the front door.

"Sir," said a voice behind us.

Andrei walked faster.

"Sir," said the voice again, louder and with an edge.

I made us both stop and we collided.

"We must pay," Andrei said.

Behind us was not the swarthy waiter who brought us the coffee but a bigger, tall blond man. His white jacket was too small for him. Over one arm he had a napkin that covered his hand. He was wearing black-and-white Reeboks, which was odd for a waiter.

Andrei let go of my arm and turned for the door. There was a sharp phut. He pitched forwards. The briefcase skidded across the floor.

I looked up at the waiter. So this is it. Run away? Legs stuck in treacle. He went past me and through the revolving door, his hand in his white jacket pocket.

Andrei lay on his back. His forehead was smooth and the Tatar's face had come through for good. From the back of his head streamed a red river of blood onto the brown marble. There was a pungent smell and I was sorry he had soiled himself. When I was out in the street I realized it was me.

I don't remember going home. I certainly didn't wait around for the police. It took me a couple of days to get over it. I stayed in the flat and shook and shouted and wept. I didn't answer the phone. Didn't let anyone in. Every few minutes I tiptoed to the hall and put my ear against the door.

Why didn't I leave? Get on the first plane home? Reason told me I was in no danger, otherwise I would already be dead. Intuition told me I had unfinished business. And a small voice, of which I was ashamed, told me that secretly I was enjoying it all.

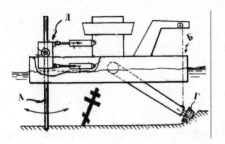

It turned out as it usually does

We were nearly there. Suppliers, equipment, staff and accounting systems were lined up. The Union would bankroll the payables and the rent for the first year. Fitting out, equipment and advertising would cost half what it would in London. We were making progress with financing. Feelers were out, grants applied for, presentations made, assurances given, intent exchanged.

The most important issue was a supply of good potatoes. Our restaurant would need 250 tons in the first year. This represented between 5 and 10 per cent of a total crop. I had secured, as well as I was able, options and contracts on seeds, storage capacity, fields and farmers, with back-up and fall-back, of almost 5000 tons. I was confident we would be able to dispose of the surplus to McDonald's or Chechens.

At last we found premises for the pilot restaurant. I had seen scores of sites, from new-build shopping centres to rat-infested *bufyets*. Afanasy introduced me to a cooperative that "owned" the Soyuz milk bar at the Kremlin end of Novi Arbat, a busy main street. Cooperatives were hangovers from the privatization of the Gorbachev era. Virtual ownership of state-owned businesses was handed over to the employees, who elected one of their number as manager. The Soyuz had gone out of business, closed down by the city sanitation department.

"Jarn, there's nuttin' wrong widdit. They wanna get their hands on the property. By no means. They owe the Union money so we got a first in."

Quite how the Union had a first in I didn't understand, however hard Afanasy tried to explain. There was no commercial legal system. Sure, there were laws, but without courts or arbitration or enforcement they were worth nothing. The validity of the Union's claim depended on how much influence they had at City Hall. The gist of Afanasy's explication was that we had enough.

The place would need remodelling. The present décor was Birmingham public lavatory circa 1965, floor-to-ceiling white tiles, green dado, terrazzo floor and neon lights. The starkness was relieved by Soviet tiling technology. In the West you start with a smooth wall and then use adhesive to stick the tiles on, with levels and plumb lines and spacers. In Russia you stick the tiles directly onto wet cement, so it's difficult to lay them flat and in straight lines. As a result a tiled wall is faceted and curvy.

The main room was just big enough for us, about twenty tables and a counter. There was a good-sized food-preparation room at the back, like a big old-fashioned scullery, with access to a yard for deliveries. The cellar was the basis of the sanitation department's decree. It was dripping with fungus and scuttling with creatures when the light turned on, but nothing that a good scrub and a few well-placed bribes could not take care of.

The cooperative could dissolve itself but not sell itself. We would have to license it or franchise it or something similar, whatever the lawyers could invent. There was no legal precedent. It was exciting, in a small way, to be adding a brick to the growing edifice of the market economy, or its ramshackle bureaucracy, depending on your point of view. My biggest concern was that the members of the cooperative should have nothing to do with the new operation. Afanasy arranged for me to meet them at the premises.

The manager was Viktor, a middle-aged man with slicked-down dyed black hair and an enormous belly hanging over the trousers of his black barathea suit and moulded into a giant Gouda by a red pullover. His face was not fat to match but almost gaunt, with what flesh it sported drooping like a beagle's, a congenitally thin man grown fat in defiance of nature. His fellow cooperatives were nine women, between 30 and 50 years old, big girls in every way, well nourished on the milk and cheeses and creams and tasty little pies they used to purvey. They circled us like a herd of curious Jerseys. I was nervous that they would bluster and bully me into taking them on, but they were intimidated by a foreigner and touchingly grateful for the pay-off, a handsome ten dollars a month each.

★

Early one morning, before eight, I was brooding over a mug of peppery coffee and planning fried eggs when the phone rang. It was Afanasy. By no means. He was outside in the square. What was he calling on? In those days the only mobiles were satellite phones. No one other than wealthy people and foreigners used them. He wanted to introduce me to someone who would help with the business. What sort of help? He wouldn't say.

I put on a jacket and tie, locked up the flat and went downstairs. As I struggled with the front-door lock I had more curious thoughts. Why had they come to the flat and not the office?

Afanasy was waiting at the bottom of the step. Behind him was a large black Mercedes sedan with tinted windows. The back door was held open by a fresh-faced youth in a bulging leather jacket, purple jogging pants and shiny white trainers. Gold on his wrist and neck glinted in the sunshine. The title on the job description of such chaps is "Bull".

"Good morning, Jarn, please…" said Afanasy, pointing to the car.

"No way, Afanasy. No way am I getting in that car."

I glanced around. It was a nice morning, but no one else was in the square. One look at our visitors and they had found urgent things to do behind their steel doors. I patted my jacket pockets.

"Ah. I forgot my business cards. I'll just go back and get them. Won't be long."

"Jarn, they know who you are. By no means. Please. It is a meeting."

★

"Whose idea was this? Are they friends of yours, Afanasy?"

He shrugged. Through bowel-trembling panic twittered the sweet voice of reason. I didn't owe them money, I wasn't in any criminal business. Drugs, gambling, prostitution, extortion, money laundering, oil, aluminium, diamonds… baked potatoes… it didn't fit. What was there to be afraid of? It could be interesting. And Afanasy was with me.

I got into the car. The bull slipped in next to me and slammed the door. Another bull was driving. His fingers were covered with the blue tattoos of Russian convicts. Afanasy waved goodbye.

As we drove through the streets the sweet voice of reason had to shout louder over the tremulous voice of my imagination. What if they weren't so clever and had got the wrong man? It crossed my mind to fling open the door and jump out, but apart from the danger of tumbling into the road I suspected the door was locked.

I attempted polite conversation, but they ignored me. I tried the gambit that has rarely failed me with men of all conditions and ranks and castes and races and backgrounds.

"What team do you support?"

"The Meat." This was less ominous than it sounds, it's the nickname of Spartak Moscow.

"Birmingham City."

"We never played you."

And that was the end of it. These were hard men.

We cruised down Leningradsky Prospekt and took the Outer Ring to the south, until we reached Gagarin Square.

We turned down Leninsky Prospekt and drove past Vladimir's Institute. A mile or so down the road we pulled up in front of a 1970s concrete building that proclaimed ГАВАНА in stark lettering. Havana. I had walked past it a couple of times on the way to Vladimir's flat. It was a Soviet-era restaurant and I had never been tempted or invited to go inside. I waited for the bulls to open the door for me and walked between them to the crinkly faux-copper door.

New Russia had come to the Havana. Dim lighting. An enormous revolving glitter ball shedding jellybean colours. A bank of blinking slot machines on the right. Whirling wheels of fortune on the left. A naked pole dancer impersonated a fireman on a stage at the far end. Men played cards or ate on tables in the middle and booths round the edges. Waitresses clothed in feather headdresses and harem pants and nothing in between bounced on high heels among them.

My bull led me to a booth occupied by a man in a dark-blue suit and open-necked white shirt, with a crucifix on a gold chain instead of a tie. He waved me to the bench at right angles to him. I sat down obediently and we sized each other up. He was a pleasant-looking chap in his early 30s, blond hair brushed forwards over his round head and nice blue eyes. His upper arms and chest inflated his suit and his bull neck filled the shirt collar. I guessed his sport was wrestling or steroids. He pointed over my shoulder and I turned to face a wobbly pair of 36Ds. I turned back to my host, unsure of what I was being offered.

"What do you wish to eat?" he asked in carefully enunciated English. "Whatever that you desire."

It was inappropriate to ask for two fried eggs, so I had scrambled.

"Mister Mule, I am pleased to make your acquaintance. My name is Barees."

"You speak excellent English."

"I made a Cambridge proficiency. It is good for my work."

"What work might that be?"

"We give service to companies."

"Do I need your services?"

"You will make your business in Novi Arbat. This comes into our responsibility."

The mafia, or brotherhood as they preferred to be called, divided Moscow into a dozen territories. Exactly how many at any one time depended on who had merged, split or been rubbed out. I wish now I had asked which family I was dealing with, how they were organized, who their competition was, how many employees they had and all the other questions I used to ask company executives when I was a bank lending officer. That would have tempered the fantasy and conjecture that filled the newspapers. But it was more prudent to speak when I was spoken to, especially as my voice had gone small and squeaky. In a mixture of equally unproficient English and Russian we clarified his terms and conditions.

"Mister Male, a business is not safe in Russia if it does not have friends. We are your friends."

"We already have a roof." I was showing off – roof is slang for protection. A cloud passed over his sunny face.

"Who is your roof?"

"The Farmers' Union. It is a governmental organization."

The sun came out again. He chuckled at what he thought was my joke.

"We make sure you will not be troubled by hooly-gons. You will have a security guard twenty-four hours. Inside and outside."

Great. A leather-jacketed bull with tattoos on his hands at the door. Very welcoming. I wondered if we could get them to wear a beefeater's costume, but now was not the time to ask.

"Why do we need you? What about the police?"

He laughed again at my joke.

"*You do not call a wolf to help you against the dogs.* The garbage are never there when you need them. And they come when they are not welcome. Let me tell you what will happen. They will come and say that according to the police regulations you must have bars on the windows at the back of the restaurant or you will have a big fine. You put in the bars. Then a fire inspector comes. He says that according to the fire regulations you must not have bars on the windows so people can escape in case of a fire. You take out the bars. Then the policeman comes back and says you must have the bars. You know they want a bribe, but how much? And different policemen come and different firemen. The city inspectors, the food inspectors, the building inspectors, the tax inspectors, the traffic inspectors… it is the same. They will bleed you dry. This is how they live. Their salaries are nothing. It is our responsibility to take care of such things. You will not have the trouble and you will save much money. We want to see your business do well."

"*The wolf hires himself out cheaply as a shepherd.*"

"Ah, you know Russian proverbs."

"The ones about wolves."

36D arrived with breakfast. Eggs for me, steak for Barees, a pot of coffee and a carafe of vodka. One of her nipples was sprinkled with breadcrumbs. I was minded to dust them off with a napkin, but thought better of it. Out of some inverted machismo it was the done thing to ignore the girls. With all this at breakfast time, what did they do for stimulation in the evening?

Barees poured and we clinked glasses. *Po paniatiam* was the toast, to our understanding.

"You have another problem. You are in the food business. You have ordered many potatoes. Yes?"

"You know a lot about our business."

"The Blacks will not like this. Vegetables is their business."

"The Blacks?"

"Our Chechen brothers. How will you get your potatoes to your shop? They will kill your drivers. They will steal your trucks. They will sell your vegetables in their markets. We will make sure you do not have a problem. We have agreements."

"So what do you charge for your services."

"10 per cent. We are very reasonable."

10 per cent. This wasn't bad at all. From what I had heard I was expecting at least double that. I made another of those jokes that he found so amusing.

"Is that 10 per cent of profit before tax or after tax?"

"Oh, Mr Meal, that is before everything." He laughed again.

"What do you mean, before everything?"

"It is very simple. At the end of the day you will give to our man 10 per cent of everything in your cash box."

"That's 10 per cent of sales."

"Of course. What did you think it was?"

He poured us another glass. I took out a pen and reached for a paper napkin. I scribbled down some numbers. Say income is 100. According to our conservative projections, all the costs would be about 80. That left profit before tax of 20. Boris's 10 per cent of sales would be 10. In other words, 50 per cent of our pre-tax profit. Leaving us 10. But we would pay tax on the 20, as mafia protection was not an allowable expense. The effective tax rate once you took into account profit tax, local tax and VAT was 90 per cent of the 20, which would come to 18. So we would make a loss of 8.

I patiently explained to Boris that 10 per cent was most unreasonable. The most we could afford would be 1 per cent. Dark clouds floated again over his sunny visage. He patiently explained the situation to me in proficient Cambridge English.

"Mr Mile, are you trying to foolish me? What is this tax? Nobody gives taxes. Nobody makes profit. Everybody make money."

"We have to account for everything to our investors and our partners. We have to keep proper books. Everything must go through the till. In England we have to account for…"

"*Do not come into another's monastery with your own Rule.*"

We were distracted by the arrival of the wine waiter, a beefy chap in a cherry-red jacket, shiny black trousers and a big gold medallion dangling over his open-necked shirt. Boris sprang to his feet and I realized I had mistaken the man's vocation. From his tan to his perfectly groomed hair to his corseted belly, everything about him was fake except for his dark eyes, so dark and expressionless they sucked in light. I had seen their sort before, in life-size photogravure on massive mobster tombstones in the German cemetery, intimidating passers-by even in death. I saw no reason to stand and devoted myself to tepid scrambled egg while he conducted a guttural conversation with Boris. He left in a jangle of jewellery and Boris sat down.

"Mister Mewel, you are very fortunate. You will have a financing of ten million roubles."

"Ten lemons? That's very gracious. We don't need it."

"How will you pay for the premises?"

"We have a joint venture with the cooperative that owns it."

"The cooperative will not make a joint venture. They will sell you the lease. We will lend you money for it."

"That is not our arrangement."

"You are mistaken."

He shrugged and refilled our glasses. They had made the cooperative a traditional non-refusable offer. They would sell us the lease and lend us the money to pay for it at a doubtless massive interest rate. In this way they laundered their money and made a safe loan to a foreign company. If we defaulted I would be killed. A good deal for them. A bad deal for me.

There was no point in arguing. We had a pleasant conversation about football while we finished our food. He was a Meat supporter too. Over a parting toast he was effusive with offers of help. He wrote down a telephone number in case I was ever in trouble. I was most grateful and charming.

We stood up. Then I did something very silly. I have done many stupid things, but this counts among the daftest. If anything can be said in my defence I would cite vodka, anger and loathing of these people and all they stood for.

"*Do svidanya,*" he said.

"Get whacked soon," I muttered, more fool me.

"Tsank you."

"I hope they cut your goolies off."

"I am pleased to meet you."

"And shove them in your gob."

"It is my pleasure."

Thank God for the limitations of the Cambridge Proficiency. He signalled to a bull loitering at the slot machines, who escorted me outside. This time the thug took me to a little BMW and got in the driver's seat himself. He was proud of the big crystal knob on the gear change. He tried to make conversation about football, but I ignored the punk and stared out of the window.

I was having nothing to do with the brotherhood. *If you make yourself a sheep you'll be eaten by the wolf.* Jackets was finished. I wanted to get out of Moscow as soon as possible. I had been naïve. I had tried to do things more or less in the same way I would do them in London. I had been living in a fantasy world. I was angry and depressed that I had not foreseen this. I had failed.

The best that could be said about the project was that it had taken me behind the news headlines into a Russia where ordinary people lived. How far? I had only scratched the surface of how things really worked. If it was any consolation, many of my Russian friends were suffering similar disappointments with the New Russia. The difference was that I had the luxury of getting on a plane while they had to stay.

It didn't take long to unwind my commitments. Malcolm was relieved, since he had his hands full with a new restaurant in Wimbledon. I had a desultory, distant phone conversation with Misha in Italy. I think he had already lost faith in Jackets, if he had ever had it. Oleg and Olga were sympathetic and Petya had never seen himself behind a counter. My fellow *rabotniks* at the Union were understanding. I sensed that they thought this would happen. I felt I had let the professor down. He was a man of great energy and integrity who worked tirelessly for his farmers and for democracy. He had been very open and supportive to us. I was a little disappointed that he seemed relieved too. The Union did not yet have the skills or experience to be an active partner in a commercial venture.

Besides, they had their hands full working on a farmers' bank with Land O'Lakes.

Afanasy was philosophical. "By no means. *We hoped for the best, but it turned out as it usually does.*"

Natasha was on holiday at her grandmother's *dacha*. I sat at her desk and wrote a letter explaining things and thanking her. I went down to say goodbye to Flor. I expected him to be disappointed in me, but his mind was on other things.

"Oh Mister John, when are you leaving Moscow? Will you be here next Friday?"

"I might be gone by then."

"What a pity."

"Why? Is there a concert?"

"I wanted to invite you to be a witness at our marriage."

"Flor, this is a great honour. Married! Congratulations! I think I will be here. Who to?"

"She did not tell you? Natasha. We handed in the application a month ago. You were in London. In Soviet Union it was three months to wait. Now it is much better."

"Natasha?" I hope I did not sound too shocked.

"You brought us together. I saw her in new light."

What light did Natasha see him in – astral? It was not an obvious match. I hoped that she perceived in him what he was, a kind and good man with just enough zaniness to keep her interested. Anyway, she had more than enough zaniness for both of them.

At the ZAGS, the registry office, there was already a procession of parties coming down the stairs when we

joined the one going up. The waiting hall was divided by
benches into a score of separate waiting areas. Different
parties were in different conditions of merriment. Those in
the one before us had to hold on to each other to make it
down the red carpet into the wedding hall. Another group
were solemn and carried bibles.

The authorities had done their best in the wedding hall
with sprays of artificial flowers and colourful banners. The
registrar was a pleasant middle-aged lady in a beige suit
who asked the usual questions and mouthed *da* to prompt
the couple. They put rings on each other's right hands and
kissed and signed the book, followed by the chief witnesses.
The registrar reminded them of their responsibilities to
each other and to the Motherland. She pressed a button on
a tape player and we walked out to Mendelssohn's wedding
march. It all took about ten minutes.

We went on a photo shoot round Moscow. When we
stopped in front of Pushkin's statue near McDonald's, I ran
and got Tomas to come and play "Sweet Georgia Brown"
for them to jive to.

After three hours of this we got back to Natasha's apartment. Her mother and grandmother were waiting for us at
the threshold with bread and salt. They had crammed
tables into the living room and hall and loaded them with
zakushka. We sat down where we could, bottles popped and
we had the first toast from Flor's friend Alexei. I was out of
my depth with his slangy Russian and in-jokes, as I was for
the rest of the toasts, which were the equivalent of the
speeches at a British wedding. But I joined in the chorus of

Za molodikh! – to the happy couple – and the chants of *Gorko, gorko.* This means "bitter" and the only thing to bring sweetness back is for the couple to stand up and kiss until they come up for air. We all counted 1…2…3…4…5 and of course it wasn't long enough so they had to do it again.

After toasts and *zakushka* the tables were pushed aside for dancing. My heart sank when one of the guests picked up an accordion, but it was all raucous and jolly enough to drown him out. My contribution to the entertainment was the first three kicks of a Cossack squatting dance and then I fell over.

It was time for me to make a toast before *shampanskoe* and vodka and the general excitement completely obfuscated my Russian. I had forgotten what I had prepared but was fluent, although unintelligible. When I had run out of things to say, I took a bulging envelope out of my pocket and asked my neighbours to pass it up the table. They weighed it in their hands and wondered if it was dollars. When it got to Flor I asked him to open it instead of putting it away with the others. He took out a sheaf of papers and handed them to Natasha, who also looked puzzled.

"Dzhorn! What are these?"

"Contracts for 5000 tons of the finest potatoes. They're all yours. *Za molodikh!*"

And that's the end of this tale.

I hope our little Russians will be happy here

t wasn't the end of the tale, though. For the next few days I moped around Moscow doing last-minute shopping and sight-seeing. Along with self-recrimination and self-doubt and self-pity and other self-centred self-indulgence was a niggling feeling of relief. Almost as inhibiting as the fear of failure is the fear of success. Did I really want to devote the next five years of my life to Russian fast food? There were so many other things to do, so many other places to see. A great weight had been lifted from my shoulders. Not least 5000 tons of potatoes.

The night before I left I had a last glass of Chablis and a cigar and went to bed early. The fax machine chattered and woke me up, but I rolled over and went back to sleep. The next morning I made a final cup of peppery coffee and finished packing. I took a farewell look around the flat, made sure the gas was turned off, peered under the bed. Like a Russian, the last thing I did before starting on my journey was to sit down quietly for a minute to let the spirit take its leave. It's

★

also the last chance to remember things like your ticket and your passport and the fax that came when you were in bed. It was from the managing director of an environmental engineering company in Lancashire. They had examined our proposal for the Bioreactor. It was ten years in advance of anything similar in Western Europe or the United States. They would like to come to Moscow and open discussions at our earliest convenience.

I cavorted round the room. I phoned Vladimir. I cancelled my ticket home. I phoned the family with the news: "This is the Big One!"

For the next year we worked hard to bring the Bioreactor to Britain. The science and technology were beyond me. My job was to mediate between English and Russian expectations and ways of doing things. For example, I had to explain to the Russians the tyranny of the Annual Budget, and to the Brits the tyranny of the Scientific Protokol. I'd written a book about this sort of thing and was pleasantly surprised to find how much of it was useful.

We made a technology transfer and licensing agreement that worked like a partnership, splitting the profits. It has survived pretty well and has just been renewed worldwide with our licensee's new American owners. Russian biochemists spent time in Wigan and British engineers in Moscow. We took a little pilot plant on a truck and plugged it into the outlet vents of prospective clients.

At last Vladimir and I stood together on the roof of a plastics factory in the Middle-Lands with the first full-size

★

Bioreactor full of bugs from Moscow. We watched the sun set over the Black Country. Carbon carmines, silicate ochres, sulphate greens, sulphide reds, sulphite greens, zinc whites and brass yellows, all burnished in the sun, the air of human industry and aspiration, ripe for remediation. The final blaze of fiery rays lit up our faces. We shook hands.

"I hope our little Russians will be happy here."

"Russians are not happy anywhere. But they get used to it."

Vladimir is now director of his Institute. With brilliance, integrity and dogged determination, he has made it an outstanding centre of research and innovation again. At the same time he has built a thriving environmental engineering company specializing in air and water treatment. Our company and our partners help to keep the air of the Shires sweet with Russian bugs.

Misha has a successful international management consultancy based in Switzerland and advises small businesses all over the world. Olga has a chain of fashion shops that Oleg helps her to manage. Flor and Natasha have two children. They live in Phoenix, where he works for a bank and she trades meteorites on the net and waits for Rapture.

A protégé of Barees bought out the cooperative and took over the restaurant. He hired a Siberian Chinese chef and fitted it out as the Hard Wok Café. About eighteen months after I left he was shot dead in his kitchen.

The Russian company Kroshka Kartoshka, Cute Little Spud, has a chain of kiosks all over Russia and Ukraine selling tasty baked potatoes and fillings. Good luck to them.